# Miss Odell:
## the Privileges of Being Present at the End of Her Life

by Connie Dunn

a reality book on caring for an elder

for my beautiful Mother, Odell Neel Jones, may she rest in peace

for my two daughters, Michelle and Erin

for my sister, Shirley

for my niece, Stacie, and her family

for my nephew, Brian

for my Aunt Emily, Mom's sister

for my wonderful and supportive wife, Joyce

for the staff at Forge Hill Senior Living

for the Season's Hospice staff

for the Circle of Care aides

for all those with dying parents

for all those with elders who want to be better prepared

and lastly...
for us all – those with good moms, great moms, and even no moms
and those with good dads, great dads, and even no dads

may this book shed light on the issues of elder care
and help you through the end

*Miss Odell: the Privileges of Being Present for the End of Her Life © 2011 Connie Dunn*

*Published by Nature Woman Wisdom*

*First Edition. Printed and bound in the United States of America.*

*All rights reserved. No part of this course may be reproduced in any form or by any electronic or mechanical means, including information storage and retrieval systems, recording, or photocopying, without permission in writing from the publisher, except by a reviewer, who may quote brief passages in review or where permitted by law.*

*Copyright © 2011 Connie Dunn*
*ISBN-13: 978-0615531953 (Nature Woman Wisdom)*
*ISBN-10: 0615531954*

*Published by Nature Woman Wisdom*

*Printed in The United States of America*

*October, 2011*
*10 9 8 7 6 5 4 3 2*

*Library of Congress Cataloging in Publication Data*
*Dunn, Connie*
     *Miss Odell: the Privileges of Being Present for the End of Her Life*
*Death*
     *Miss Odell: the Privileges of Being Present for the End of Her Life*
     *by Connie Dunn*
*Elders*
     *Miss Odell: the Privileges of Being Present for the End of Her Life*
     *by Connie Dunn*
*Spiritual*
     *Miss Odell: the Privileges of Being Present for the End of Her Life*
     *by Connie Dunn*

# Butterfly Momma

*Butterfly Momma*

Sleep, Momma, sleep! You are tired.
Go into your cocoon, Momma, sleep.
You are too tired to swallow;
Too tired to talk. Shhh, Momma. I love you.

"I love you, forever," Momma said to me.
"I love you, forever, my sweet Momma."
And she smiled, closed her eyes and slept.
How many days? How many nights? Who knows?

I sat vigil at her bedside.
My heart said, "hold on. I need you."
But I knew in my head that
Momma couldn't stay forever on this earth.

It's time, sweet Momma, to feel your wings,
And fittingly so, they were Butterfly Wings.
She loved butterflies and so did I.
No more sleeping for my Butterfly Mom.

She can flit here and there – from flower to flower.
My Butterfly Mom in her beautiful wings
Will sing with chorus, spreading love everywhere
While I wipe my tears of sorrow and loss.

Sleep, Momma, sleep! You are tired.
Go into your cocoon, Mamma sleep.
You are too tired to swallow;
Too tired to talk. Shhh, Momma. I love you.

"I love you forever," Momma said to me.
"I love you forever, my sweet Momma:"
And she smiled, closed her eyes and slept.
The angels were around her, they filled her room.

She took one last breath and the room emptied.
Her Butterfly Wings took her into the light,
And there she will always be
Among the flowers and the trees.
- Connie Dunn

# TABLE OF CONTENTS

Introduction .................................................................. 7
Elder Care .................................................................. 19
Light Beings ............................................................... 25
Miss Odell .................................................................. 33
Miss Odell, My Mother ............................................... 41
Miss Odell's Elder Care .............................................. 53
How to Navigate the Finances .................................. 61
Keeping Family Tuned-in ........................................... 69
How to Move an Elder ............................................... 81
How to Find Appropriate Housing ............................. 97
What Services Are Available? .................................. 108
When Life Leaves, Then What? ................................ 113
The Mourning ............................................................ 119
About the Author ...................................................... 133

Left Back: Sarah Jane Marchbanks, Shirley Ann Jones (Clark), Olivia Marchbanks Neel, Odell Neel Jones, Front: Connie Dell Jones (Dunn)

# INTRODUCTION

## *End of Life*

The end of life is inevitable for each of us. Though we fight it or embrace it, we cannot control the time or day. We can be patient or uneasy with the ideas of death and dying, but it does not change our fate.

Throughout time, people have searched for a solution. The United States of America might not have even been discovered for many hundreds of years were it not for Ponce de Leon's search for the Fountain of Youth. During the 16$^{th}$ Century, there were many such myths and legends about the miracle waters that could restore youth or keep you from aging.

Unfortunately, these are simply myths and legends. The Fountain of Youth did not exist then or now. People grow old and die. While Americans have some issues with aging and dying, death is part of life. We live with that expiration date unrevealed. The truth of the matter is that our bodies wear out. To live forever would be too painful! As I get older, I realize that death is not something that we should fear but welcome cautiously. I'm not suggesting that we choose to commit suicide to leave this life, but approach death with understanding. Values for living and dying are important aspects of comprehending the finite boundaries of our human existence.

I write this book not as a book about how to die, but a book about living until the end. I am only an observer on this path at the moment, or so I am convinced. I wait at the bedside of my mom. But though some days are difficult for her, many are filled with all the love that she has exuded throughout her 92 ½ years of life.

## Mom and End of Life

Rev. Mike, a minister that holds church services at the assisted living facility where Mom lives says, "Your mom's a special person. She has a special gift."

He went on to tell me about a multi-colored doily that Mom had made and given him. He so treasures it that it sits on his altar with his Communion Cup and Anointing Oil. Rev. Mike is right: Mom does have a special gift. She has a generous and compassionate spirit. She gives from her heart and she always has – all her life.

Mom is ready to go. I, on the other hand, am not quite ready for her departure. But what child can really prepare for that at any age?

As I begin this writing project, I have received a call about my mom. Her heart is racing and she is having difficulty breathing. This is her congestive heart failure at work. Will she pull through yet another episode? My gut says, yes. But my heart is saddened, because with each episode, I know she grows weaker.

Just yesterday, we sat with crochet needles in hand as she taught me the stitches to a scarf I wanted to make. Even at the end of one's life, you have value. I want my mom to feel that. When she feels well enough to work, we work. When she does not, we don't.

Why do I feel it is a privilege to be present at the end of her life? It's like celebrating her life every time I see her. Every moment is precious. It reminds me of when my youngest child was born. Everyone told me how special it is to have a newborn baby and to cherish each moment with her. They were right. It seems ironic that at the beginning and end of life, we treasure life in such a unique way that there are some similarities.

I cannot determine if this is just a mother-daughter bonding thing, but I believe it to be deeper and more meaningful. When a new soul arrives on the planet, their eyes are windows to our world. Soft voices, loving eyes, and sweet caresses are what newborns need. Not that every newborn gets this treatment. I cannot even tell you that my sweet, baby girl that I gave birth to got this treatment. I had two older adopted children, which did have some impact on that. It was my only opportunity to have and hold a living soul that came from my body. That was intense and unreal at the same time. While the baby is in the womb, it's hard to imagine them in real time, because life is swirling around you, as well. Once they come out, they begin commanding attention. Yet, there is sweetness about their baby needs.

Here I am with my mom, neither of us are newborns. Both of us have been around awhile. As the end of her life grows closer, I marvel at her tenacity and see through her awareness of something that comes after this life.

Maybe I've been a bit skeptical of any afterlife in the past. After all, it's hard to believe in something that is so intangible. Sitting vigil in Mom's room has taught me quite a few things. First, death is not the end. Second, *Light Beings* or *Angels* are real. Thirdly, there are many stages to dying. Some people take weeks or months. Others can do all the stages in one day. My fourth realization was that we do have some control over leaving this world. Maybe this is not total control, but even some control is better than the norm.

We cannot know without a doubt the moment of our death. Yet, when we are born, we surely will die. From the moment of birth, we are growing toward our own demise. Is this the reason that humankind developed religion? Perhaps…and then…maybe it is just our need for establishing meaning to our life or somewhere in between.

## Why I Chose this Book Project

I began this book project as a way for me to capture and appreciate my mom's end of life. It's not something that you plan how you're going to get through it. In fact, we usually avoid thinking about our parents' death. Death is final in our minds; and no matter how old we are when our parents' reach this stage, we, as children, are not ready to lose them. We can be practical and logical about it, but totally ready? No. The only ones who could be ready and willing to lose their parent is a child who doesn't understand love or received none in her or his life.

There are not instruction manuals to prepare us for the end of life just like there are no guides for raising kids. You are basically on your own to figure it all out. Fortunately, I have lived long enough to have lost people that I love. It wasn't my precious mom, but they were important people in my life, as well.

My grandfather was the first. I remember seeing him after his death many, many times...or so I thought I did. Quite a few years later, one of my aunts committed suicide. It was tragic. It was difficult for everyone. There is little you can hold on to when someone takes their life. It's as if they robbed you of closure, because you didn't know they were going die. But this is a feeling some people have no matter how one leaves this earth! Many years later, my grandmother passed, followed by another aunt. Both aunts were my mom's sisters. Both grandparents were my mom's parents. Many more years later, my dad's parents passed. Because I never felt like I knew this set of grandparents, it was harder to mourn their loss. Mourning is a natural process, but it was difficult to feel that about two people related to me that I hardly knew. They basically were strangers, although growing up we visited them yearly.

Again, this is not a book about dying, because I don't think I could tell anyone anything about how to die. I'm still very much among the living! And I plan to stay that way for quite some time. What I can tell you is how to be there for the person who is dying. I never knew I could do this. And maybe I couldn't have even a year ago.

Knowing that you can be strong for someone shouldn't be taken lightly. If Mom wasn't so sure about being ready to die, I'm not sure I could be as strong. This is not the same as being immune to what happens. When the time comes for her to die, I will be sad, and I will miss her. However, I know that I won't fall apart, because that just isn't who I am.

It's an honor to accompany my mom on this earthly journey. I know it's a conscious choice to be there for her. I cannot continue with her, but that, too, is a choice. Most loved ones aren't asking anyone to pass with them, but be there on the final voyage of their life. I can do that for her. I can love her through to the end. I can do my Reiki on her to help her be strong. I can hold her hand, rub her cheeks, and kiss her forehead. I can keep her as hydrated, as possible. I can keep her comfortable and pain free, but I cannot pass over to the other side with her. It is not my time. I'm okay with that. I have lots to do with the rest of my life.

## Tough Questions and Thoughts on Death

What happens when a person dies? This is the adventure that you can only make after you have passed into the Spirit World, Heaven, or whatever you want to call the afterlife. Some people don't believe in a life after death. I honor that opinion. But if I ever had any doubts about the existence of something after death, I certainly have no doubt about it now.

The phenomenon of *Angels* and *Spirits* and *Light Beings* exist. I feel their presence. Mom tells me that they are here with her and it's not quite her time. She does ask me when the 9th is? August 9 is my mom and dad's wedding anniversary. On August 9, my mom and dad would have been married 69 years. My mom loved my dad. It was a very strong, loving bond on her part. She only saw the best in my dad! She believes that he will come for her. I can only smile lovingly and tell her how romantic that is. I can also tell her that if Dad comes for you, it is okay to go.

Giving her permission to leave is often important to those who are nearing the end of their life. They want to know you will be okay. They want you to know that they will stay with you, if they need to. But that seems cruel to ask of my mom, I couldn't be that selfish. I can see her body is just wearing out. I know I cannot keep her with me forever. But I can also help her live to the fullest capacity she can, each day she is on this planet.

## *A Bit About this Book and Miss Odell*

This book is about Miss Odell. She is my mom and I call her Miss Odell here, because so many people have called her that. She's the epitome of a fine Southern lady. In the Deep South, which isn't necessarily just Texas or Tennessee, calling someone "Miss" is a sign of respect. It doesn't really reflect their marital status, but just that they command a certain amount of admiration.

When Mom had ladies coming in around the clock to care for Dad and her, they called her Miss Odell. This book is about Miss Odell, you'll be getting to know her better. She is a kind and gentle, sweet person. Although she has had a lot of pain in her elder years with hip replacements, arthritis, and osteoporosis – in particular, her neck area – she's never gotten bitter or mean. Mom retains her loving personality.

She is the Sweet Southern Lady that she has always been: too polite to let people know how much she really hurts. It's the heart pain lately that worries me. Her heart beats hard trying to pump blood to the rest of her body due to her congestive heart failure. She now feels that on a fairly regular basis. I understand it well – too well! My youngest, Erin, has arrhythmia that causes her heart to beat hard; and she, too, feels that pain. I can see their hearts beating hard and can feel it, as well. Erin is only 23. Her youth helps her cope better.

In this book, I will be sharing stories about Mom. We are all fortunate that Mom decided to write about her life as a way to share with her grandchildren, which means that some of my stories will give her a voice, as well. While this book is not a chronological biography, I hope the stories help you know her spirit. That is really my goal, as well as to impart the journey of her end of life in a way that I hope helps you with the elder in your life.

## *How the Book is Structured*

This book is broken into 13 Chapters, including this introduction. *Elder Care* defines this term and how it affects us all, even those who are not primary caregivers.

The *Light Beings* chapter discusses *Angels, Spirits,* and *Light Beings*. I start with this chapter, because out of all of the experiences that I had with Mom, this was probably the most rewarding, comforting, and surprising.

There are three chapters devoted to Mom: *Miss Odell, Miss Odell, My Mother,* and *Miss Odell's Elder Care*. I tried to write as much about what was important in these three definite time periods and relationships. *Miss Odell* is more about Mom and Dad in their early years. *Miss Odell, My Mother* highlights some of the wisdom that she passed on to Shirley and I. *Miss Odell's Elder Care* speaks for itself. It is where I talk about her care both in Tennessee and in Massachusetts.

The rest of the book will have stories about Miss Odell or some experiences that I had with Mom that relate to the individual topics. *How to Navigate the Finances* is a chapter about how you can approach the finances of your elder. This can be a tricky situation, and even though your intentions are good, your loved one might be very resistant.

*Keeping Family Tuned-In* is about keeping your siblings in the loop of what's happening. This chapter discusses some of the important communication issues that become your responsibility when you are the primary caregiver.

*How to Move an Elder* is about moving a large distance or even shorter with your elder. There are some things that I learned by moving Mom over a thousand miles, which may be helpful if you find yourself in a similar position. Even, if you don't have to move that distance, it may be helpful to learn how to go about such a move.

*How to Find Appropriate Housing* is just that. There are some non-profit organizations that will help you no matter where you are looking for elder care housing. While no one can truly make that decision but you, I have attempted to give you some guidelines that will help.

*What Services Are Available* will discuss many options that you might find or need. Because there are different titles given to some of the people for which you contract, I've discussed what it is that each different type of caregiver offers. In this way, I hope you are able to move forward with more knowledge.

*When Life Leaves, Then What?* is about what happens in the end. Since I have only begun this journey, I have no idea what this chapter will be. That rests in the unknown.

*The Mourning* is the last chapter. It is about grief, the stages of grief, and the process of grief. While as I write this, I don't know how I will handle mourning my mom, so the last two chapters are more of a mystery to me.

Odell Neel and Evelyn Neel

We all start out as babies and children, but we grow up and grow old. It is the human condition.

Left back: Susan, Beulah
Left middle: Bell, Jewel, Frankie, Madeline, Olivia*
Left front: Sarah Marchbanks (mother of all these daughters)

*Olivia Marchbanks Neel – mother of Miss Odell

# ELDER CARE

An elder is someone who is older than you, according to dictionary definitions. Having said that, I use this term and senior interchangeably throughout this book referring to someone who is probably over the age of 80, because people are living longer and healthier these days. Your elder could be younger or older, but probably the reason you are involved in their care is due to some health issues, usually long-term illnesses or disabilities.

There are so many issues that elders face. While the American Disabilities Act has done a lot to make the world more accessible, it really is an inaccessible world for so many people. For example, doctor's offices often have a ramp to get into the building. But if it doesn't open automatically, your elder will need a good deal of help getting into the building. In fact, taking my mom in a wheel chair to the doctor required that I call and get some assistance. There was no way to open the door and hold onto the chair. The platform was so short and the door opened outward.

Most of the doctor's offices we visited had similar issues. If there wasn't someone there to help, you really couldn't get in. Even when Mom was on a walker there were issues with the logistics of getting her into a building. I often felt like I needed several more hands and arms.

We coped and others do, as well, but the fact is that access is important to elders. Even living in an assisted living facility had its limitations. She was never going to be able to go on their bus for field trips or shopping or doctor's office visits. The bus had steps up into it. While there was someone to help her, they would have had to literally pick her up and put her into the bus. We just chose not to use the bus, because I did her shopping and took her to doctor's visits.

When elders need a change in housing, it comes up quickly. Their needs can literally change over night. Something small can happen and change their whole world. Elders can exhibit dementia by communicating fears. This does not mean that they are demented. It could be that the fears are real or that they need attention. It does mean that you may need to intervene to assess their situation.

Assessments can be done in several ways. If you live close by, you can observe. You can take them to a doctor for evaluation. You can get a social worker from an elder affairs organization to do an assessment. Unfortunately, elder services do vary from state-to-state and sometimes from city-to-city/town-to-town.

Elder care also may require some legal papers. Things like wills, powers of attorney and health care proxies are standard requirements. If you move your elder out of state, you may need to get the will updated for the state your elder is now living in.

Who should have the power of attorney? The person who is handling the finances needs the power of attorney. The health care proxy should go to the person who is doing the care giving. Sometimes this is the same person.

One of the harder issues would be if you need to declare your elder as unfit to handle their own affairs. When our Mom was in Tennessee, we considered this option, because we thought she was becoming demented. Her money was flying out of her account.

What Shirley (sister) and I finally came to is that we didn't want to go the court route. We didn't want to do that to our mom. On the other hand, we would have done this if our attempt to move her had fallen through.

I see my mom every day, but my sister lives on the opposite coast and can only be here for one week a year. There are issues surrounding elders that cannot be avoided. Having good discussions around death are important. Understanding what legal papers you need to have in place are simply the beginning. And if there are no legal papers in place, that is certainly your first step.

Yes, it's not a light supper topic for discussion. However, you need to know what the wishes are of your mother, father, grandparent, etc. Will there be a wake or a funeral or both? Will there be a graveside service? And do you even have a burial plot? How do you pick a funeral home?

The dartboard style choices you see available may not sit well on your palate. Do not worry: your parent(s) or other elder may already have decided what they want. If you have chosen or fallen into the caregiver of your particular elder, these are not optional discussions. You must know their wishes. You may even have to explore some options with them in order to help them make hard decisions about their death. You also need to make sure all the legal paperwork is in place, such as a will, power of attorney, and health care proxy. Without these legal devices, you may find that medical professionals, legal council, or banks cannot discuss your elder's case or files or whatever.

When you have conversations about what your elder wishes to happen, you may discover that your loved one has thought about these issues deeply and logically. For example, my sister and I were surprised to find out that my dad was being cremated when he passed. We were surprised, because it seemed like such a modern choice.

Mom wants the same thing, so it's relatively easy. Neither wanted a funeral. In truth, there would be few people, who are still alive and living in Tennessee, to attend a funeral. In Waco, Texas, there would be a few more. Mom would have cousins that would likely attend. Here in Massachusetts, only the people in her assisted living facility know her. She's not been well enough to come to church with me. It's hard on Mom to get in and out of the car. It just wears her out, and she needs to rest a lot.

While I consider it a privilege to be on this journey with my mom, I would prefer that she would never reach that end. The problem with that sort of thinking is that I can see how worn out she gets. Just bending over to put on her shoes makes her totally out of breath, which makes me understand that her congestive heart failure is advancing. If I could breathe for her, I would.

Life is often hard. We all face challenges of one degree or another. I have psoriatic arthritis, so I know a thing or two about pain. As a healer, I also know that if we can sort of short circuit the pain center, we can help to diminish the pain. Sometimes it's just temporary, but relief for a few minutes at a time is still relief. I also know that energy healing can repair some things on some people and not at all on others. In other words, healing energy has a mind of its own; and you can only do what the life force energy chooses to do. Sometimes that means that you cannot fix the problem, but the Reiki energy may help the person deal with the emotions of not fixing the problem.

Is there pain involved in death? That is one of the big questions about the end of life that we cannot answer globally. I think that it doesn't have to be. Hospice's goal is to keep people comfortable during this time. Mom does not suffer. She can be kept totally pain-free. My goal is to help Mom have a peaceful and painless passing.

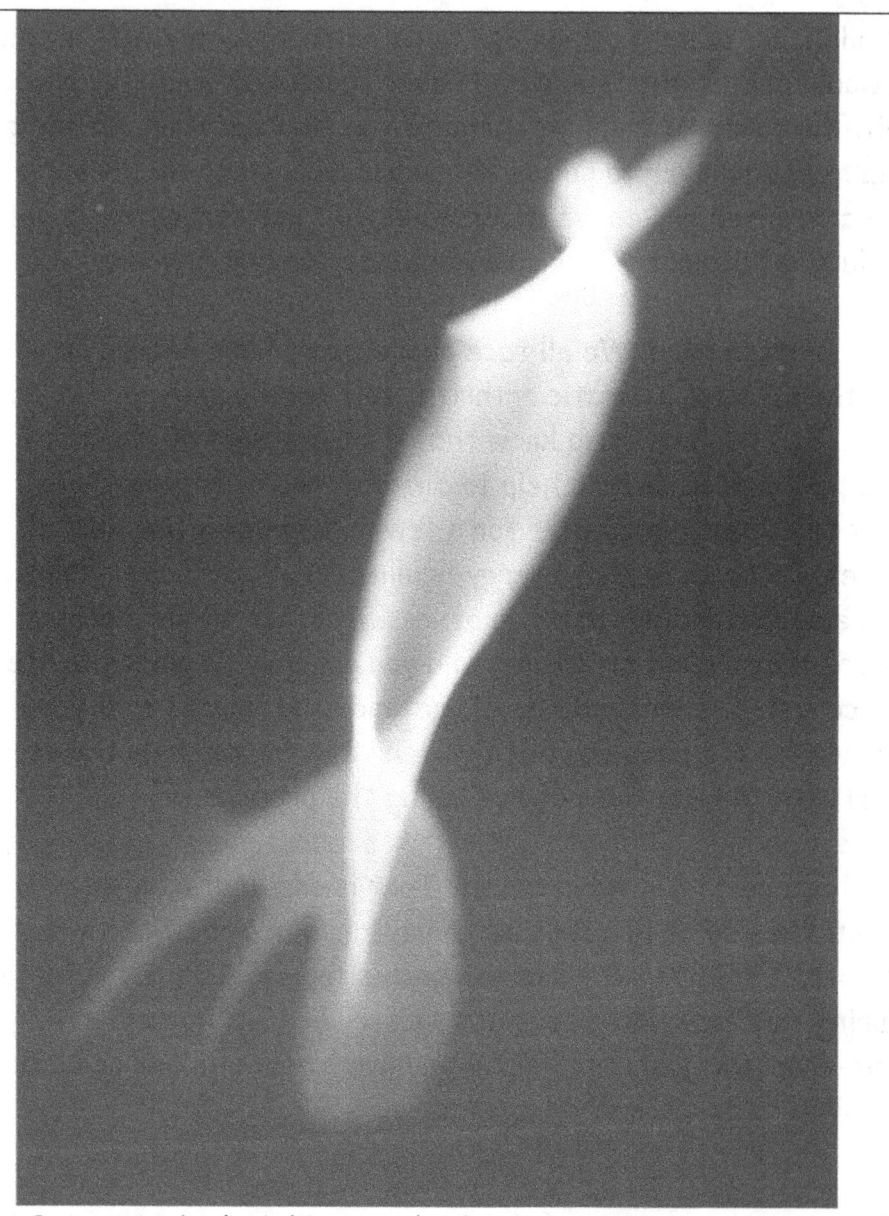

Light Beings might look like angels, fairies, spirits or just orbs of light.

# LIGHT BEINGS

Each of us is simply energy, which is often expressed as light. Our life force energy can be seen as light. As an Energy Healer, I sense energy or feel the energy. Through my third eye (forehead), I can see colored light emitting from people for whom I am doing a healing session. Light Beings are what I call Ascended Beings. Some people would call them Angels or Spirits. Whatever you want to call them, they appear as White Light.

While no one knows for sure what happens at the end of our life, there have been enough people with near death experiences to believe that our life force energy or soul leaves our body and floats toward a light source. This light source is an unknown, as far as I can tell. Those life force energy entities don't come back from there to tell us what that light source is. We can use our imaginations to come to some ideas about what the source is. I think of it as a community of Light Beings. Some people might say that was Heaven and that the Light Beings are Angels. And I would say that there is little difference in these descriptions but more in the expression of them.

Are there Light Beings that walk with us day-to-day? Probably! That would explain those times when you took the wrong exit and had you not, you might have been involved in a big accident. Guardian angels, some folks call them. But we don't really know the entire scope of Light Beings, nor shall we until we pass on to that place. Many folks don't even believe in such things. Is it right or wrong? Only you can decide for yourself.

There have been many times lately when I've sensed an energy presence without another human in the room or, at least, not one that is awake and walking around. My tiny Chihuahua, Rusty, sees them, I believe. He stares at things intently sizing them up.

This can be freaky for some people, but being able to sense the energy, I can tell that these Light Beings are good. If here is an opposite of these Light Beings, I have been fortunate not to have sensed any. I would like to believe that energy is pure and good just as the Universe is a good Universe.

My sister, who leans more towards disbelief in most things, has also had encounters of the Light Beings. She described it as a purple haze and an urgent feeling about our mother. She said that she thought it was our father telling her to go help our mother. At that time, there were problems with our mom's care in rural Tennessee.

I again encountered a room full of Light Beings one night while caring for Mother. It was somewhat strange and awesome at the same time. Rusty (my tiny Chihuahua) was seeing something. Mother was talking to them. I felt their presence. She may have been talking to my dad. It was hard to discern, some of what she was experiencing. It was obvious she was dreaming but busy. She tried to get out of bed several times. Finally, she settled down, but the room still felt crowded with Light Beings.

I remembered feeling intrigued by this even though I was writing on this book. I stopped writing and observed the room, putting myself in a state of meditation. I could sense numerous Light Beings. I couldn't communicate with them, but I was aware of their presence.

When I asked my mom the next day, she said they were all angels. She also said that our dad was there. He wanted her to go with him. She didn't go. The angels sent her back. It wasn't quite her time. She asked me when August 9 was? I told her Tuesday. That was Thursday.

Light Beings or Angels seem to hang out in assisted living facilities and nursing homes, so I understand. The aides and, in particular, the hospice nurses, have witnessed this phenomenon numerous times. Are they angels of death? There may be an angel of death, but I see these Light Beings as guides into the light community or heaven, as some people interpret that.

There are a lot of ways to understand Light Beings. Angels, Spirits, Light Beings, and maybe even Fairies, as well, can all be interchangeable. The big question in your mind might well be, how do we access the power of these Light Beings? That's both easy and complicated. You see, Light Beings find you rather than the reverse. Having said this, I feel strongly that if you are open to the Light Beings, they will reveal themselves to you when you are ready to receive them.

Spiritual development is one way to help you join the Light Being World. There are many ways to develop one's spirituality. Practicing consistent spiritual practices are among the top ways to develop your spiritual self. Taking a spiritual journey or setting off on a voyage inward are also good ways to develop your spiritually. In particular, you need to have the intent of deepening your spirituality. And if your goal is to just capture a Light Being and grabbing their power, then you are very misguided and will most surely fail.

The power of Light Beings, as I have experienced it is, is not the same power that we think of in our real world. Power in the Light Being world is much more esoteric. When we think of power in our human sort of way, we actually think along the lines of money, political, and dominance. In the Light Being World, I think it is more about intensity and capacity for love. Love equals power might be a good equation for the Light Being World.

On another occasion, I found Angels (could be Light Beings, but since my mom had said they were angels, I chose to go with that) watching over mom. The room was filled with them. I had seen them as Light Beings before, but today, it was clear that they were Angels. I also felt the presence of my dad and my grandparents (my mom's parents). I had the distinct feeling there was a very large Light Being of importance standing at the head of Mom's bed. I felt it must be Jesus or another male Light Being in charge and larger than life. I wasn't scared or worried by the impression but more comfortable knowing that the gathering of Angels and Spirits were being orchestrated by some wonderful and awesome presence.

You see, it really isn't about me. It is all about my mother. She has always been a generous giver of love and light. So thinking of the Light Beings as Angels didn't really cause me any hardships. I do have a different image of Angels than Light Beings. Whereas, the Light Beings are definitely white lights, the Angels seem to be a bit more definitive with wings and white glowing robes. I'm sure that my childhood image is what is causing me to imagine Angels in this way. It really doesn't matter what my image of Angels are, because this is really all about Mom!

Mom has been a bit restless, so I decide to do a little Reiki. She smiles and looks up at me and says, "That's what I needed...for you to put your hands on me."

I am surprised to find it difficult to get into my Reiki mode. Perhaps, it is that the sun is shining brightly in Mom's room. I suppose I usually do Reiki in a dimly lit room with maybe a candle or two burning. Music is also missing. I often rely on the music to take me deep into my Reiki trance. Of course, because this is my mom, it does make sense that I might be a bit too emotionally attached to get into that Reiki state of just being and holding the energy. While I think I'm calm and in control, I may actually be experiencing more internal stress than I think or will admit to myself. After all, my mom is very sick, probably the sickest she's ever been. I swore I was strong and could take it, but maybe the little girl in me still wants her mommy to get better. I do find solace in simply sitting in the room with her. And I enjoy the opportunity to sit with my thoughts and write them on my computer.

With each day, I find the room is filled with Angels and Light Beings. It is comforting. It is peaceful. I am in the presence of such strong, peace-loving energy. It feels like love is filling the room with all these Light Beings. I wonder at that thought. Is it my love or my mom's love? Hmmm. I suppose that could be either or both. Mom is naturally loving, and I'm loving my mom through this time. While I could over analyze this, I decide that it doesn't matter why or how the Light Beings and Angels are there, it simply is wonderful that they are!

Light Beings or lightworker? There are some similarities. The Light Beings are, in general, Spirits and Angels. The lightworker is someone who works with the Light Beings on behalf of another. Communicating with a Light Being is a gift. People who are lightworkers do readings. They are partially psychic and partially telepathic, which explains the mode of communication. Lightworkers help people know their Angels or Light Beings. Clairvoyant people have these abilities.

There are some ways to help you to develop clairvoyance. We all have energy centers down our spine, which are called Chakras. Beginning at your tail bone, you have a Base, Sacral, Solar Plexus, Heart, Neck, Third Eye, and Crown Chakras. It is the Third Eye Chakra that helps your inner seeing. If you don't think about seeing in the same way you see with your eyes, the process is a bit easier. When you see with your Third Eye, you can start by picturing an event or a place for which you've actually experienced. When you can recreate a scene you know, then you can notice where it is in your body that you sense the scene. For example, is there a movie screen? If so, where is it? How does that relate to your other senses? These are the parts that are most important when you are being clairvoyant.

Sensing another person's presence without seeing them is very much like being clairvoyant. When you feel that energy, you must still go a bit farther to communicate with it. I suggest baby steps are best. Communication is the most complicated, because that implies a conversation. However, you may not get a whole conversation; you may only hear what the Light Being wants you to hear. Perhaps, you won't have a conversation but rather feel an overwhelming peace.

Angel Readings are popular. They usually involve a conversation with the person for whom you are doing the reading. You have to verify that what you are sensing fits into a reality for your client. Interpreting what you sense can be the hardest part.

While I have experienced clairvoyance to a small degree, I cannot claim to have communicated at all. I've only sensed their presence or size or both. There's a long way to go before I can communicate with these Light Beings or Angels. I'm not totally sure that this is even part of my path.

I am sure of their existence. Beautiful shimmering white light exudes from them. Wings protruding from their back, Angels stand ready at the watch of those who are nearing their end of life on earth.

It is finite, this life of ours. It begins in a breath and ends with one. It is comforting to know that Angels and Light Beings are there to help us transition from this earthly life to our next life.

Olivia and Sidney Neel
Miss Odell's Parents

# MISS ODELL

Miss Odell was the first born daughter of a cotton farmer and a homemaker. Sidney and Olivia, her parents, went on to have three more daughters. Like most farming families of the era, they made their lives from the dirt. They scratched out a living in Central Texas, farming cotton, raising their vegetables, chickens and eggs, pigs, and a milk cow. They had a smoke house where they smoked their meats. They had a root cellar where they kept the potatoes and other vegetables as fresh as possible and stored their canned goods, such as beans, corn, pickles, tomatoes and other vegetables grown. They also canned their own jellies and jams.

Miss Odell grew up with all the skills to run her own home. She learned to can, grow vegetables, clean, sew, and take care of the kids. She was raised to be a homemaker for which was all a woman in the early 1900s could aspire.

When Miss Odell was a teenager, her desire was to be a County Extension Agent, which would require a degree in home economics. She would go around to the different farms and teach the women to can, pickle, and make jams and jellies. It was an acceptable career for a woman like being a librarian. But there was no money for college for Miss Odell.

Hard times fell to the Neel family, and the farm didn't last. Cotton crops fail, bills mount, and there were probably a lot of reasons that the farm had to be sold. When Miss Odell was 10, they lost the farm. Living in the city, Sidney became a carpenter; Olivia became a seamstress, maker of drapes, and reupholstering furniture.

After graduating from high school, Miss Odell went to work for Frankie's Bakery in Waco, TX. She was taught how to put the icing/frosting (in the south, icing is the preferred word; however, in the north frosting is used) on the cake. A young man, named Harold Jones, worked for his uncle, George O. Jones who owned the bakery. Harold's job was to grease the cake pans. Well, the two met and began to date. Later, they married on August 9, 1942. War had broken out in Europe and the US joined forces for World War II.

Harold got leave at Christmas the first year they were married. Miss Odell stayed home with her mother and dad and worked. She saved all she could. By February, Harold was stationed in one place, so he sent for his bride. He was at Ft. Sheridan, Illinois, just outside of Chicago. They rented a room in an Italian home. They didn't have a kitchen, so they had to eat out a lot. However, the Lenzi family from whom they rented invited them to dinner every Sunday.

Miss Odell found a job right away at the Ft. Sheridan PX café as a waitress. With the tips and salary, she and Harold scraped by and Miss Odell was able to eat a lot of her meals there. I remember my mom saying, "We would do anything so we could be together, because we loved each other so very much. Very few couples had the deep love we had for each other."

Miss Odell's feet bothered her from standing on them and waitressing. The doctor diagnosed arthritis. Miss Odell wasn't used to the severe cold and snow that Chicago, Illinois, dished out over the winter. Miss Odell changed jobs; she went to work at Weibolts, a large department store in North Chicago. Miss Odell says, "I worked with the manager of the sportswear department and I checked advertising, took inventory to be sure we had the merchandise for the ad by the time it came out in the paper. I also used a slide ruler to keep up to date averages for sales of each part of the department each day."

Another four or five months, Miss Odell discovered she was pregnant, and the ride on the elevated railroad from Highwood to North Chicago made her so nauseas that she decided to find a job somewhere else. Miss Odell found that new job from a newspaper ad. She went to work for Amature Company in their payroll department.

But there was a war going on, and Miss Odell and Harold would have to split up again. They had been together almost a year. Harold had leave and drove Miss Odell home in the Plymouth with all her extra clothes and baby clothes and things that had accumulated. Harold took Miss Odell to Waco, Texas, to live with her mother and father. By that time, she was about four-and-a-half months along in the pregnancy.

Miss Odell and Harold hated to say goodbye, but in the army, you don't exactly have any choices! In June, Harold got another leave when Shirley Ann was to be born. But she was late, so Harold had to send a telegram for an extension of his leave. Luckily, he hung on to the telegram giving him permission to extend the leave. When Harold returned to camp, they had marked him A.W.O.L. (absent without leave). It turned out okay, but it was pretty messy for Harold.

Shirley was born on Flag Day, June 14, 1944. She was a tiny little baby; and what hair she had was blonde. The nurses all called her "Betty Grable." Shirley's eyes were blue like her dad and her grandfather Neel. There were other blue-eyed people in Miss Odell's family. Both Emily and Evelyn had blue eyes, as well. Everyone else had brown eyes.

When Shirley was three months old, Miss Odell was still nursing her. However, Harold found out he was being sent overseas with the 194th General Hospital group. He wanted to see Miss Odell, but he couldn't come home. So, Miss Odell packed her bag with mostly baby stuff, bundled up Shirley, and took a pillow to lay her on to sleep. Off she went to Rockford, Illinois, on the train.

They used a dresser drawer as a basinet for Shirley. Miss Odell and Harold were proud parents and eagerly showed her off at several parties with friends and other army wives. Harold loved seeing Shirley, too. They were the only one with a baby. Naturally, everywhere they went, Shirley went, as well.

For that short stay, they lived in a home where four couples shared the kitchen and had certain times to cook and eat. A lot of foods were rationed, but they managed. Miss Odell said, "Being together was so worth it! He had to leave then. Goodbyes were harder than ever. After he left, I shed a lot of tears."

The couple who owned the house were nice folks, they took Miss Odell to the train. Harold's folks lived in St. Louis, so Miss Odell stopped there so they could see their new granddaughter, Shirley Ann. Mildred, Harold's sister also got to meet Shirley. Then, Miss Odell returned to Waco.

Harold and Miss Odell wrote each other every day. Sometimes Miss Odell would get several letters at a time. She would send him pictures of Shirley as she was growing. Harold was the head of the cooking unit of the 194th General Hospital in Paris, France. He was stationed overseas 17 months, before the war was over.

In the meantime, Miss Odell lived in her parent's house. They rented out half the house for quite a few years. Her mother and dad were at Los Alamos, New Mexico, where Sidney was working as a skilled carpenter. Miss Odell and Harold were living together once again. Shirley Ann was not as enamored of the living arrangements. Miss Odell had taught her that her dad was the picture – well, maybe that wasn't her intent. However, Shirley had to get adjusted to her daddy as the man that was now living in their house.

Harold and Miss Odell did not have a car, but now that Harold was no longer away, they felt they needed one. At this time, there were no new cars available. Harold, Miss Odell, and Shirley went car hunting. "No new cars were out so soon after the war," said Miss Odell, "so we found a second-hand Hudson, which looked good."

Would you believe it? They no sooner got the car home to take it on a spin, when Harold tried to shift gears. The whole mechanism came off in his hand. Harold told this story at a Toastmaster's group. The story was very funny! And it was also a true story.

Harold was able to get the car fixed. And he was also able to find a job in the meat department of one of the local Safeway Stores. This helped them get by financially. Miss Odell's mother and dad had returned home from Los Alamos, New Mexico. Miss Odell and Harold moved into the two-room apartment on the other side of the house. Harold started to 4C College night school. Later, he went to work for the Texas Company later known as Texaco.

Not too much later, Miss Odell and Harold moved to Blackland Air Force Base, which had closed after the end of the war. The barracks buildings were made into apartments.

Miss Odell says, "We bought our first furniture, a living room suit, which was a maroon couch and chair, plus a blue platform rocker; a dinette set, which was red and white; and one bedroom set. We had signed up to get a G.E. refrigerator before we left Mother and Dad's house. It was so good to have a place of our own; we lived there for almost a year before we started looking for a home closer to his work. We found a nice place at 1220 Ashleman Street in Bellmead, close to Waco.

"The Ashleman house had four rooms and a bath with a separate garage and was painted white outside. It was closer for Harold, because he worked at Texaco on Dallas road, which was about a mile away," she explains.

Miss Odell loved it there. They started a garden. They even had a back yard that was fenced in. They were really happy there, says Miss Odell. "And when we moved there, I found out I was pregnant.

"Connie Dell was born after one of the worst winters we'd had in a long time. On March 15, 1949, she was born," says Miss Odell. "She was such a happy, lovable baby and her Dad got to rock her and be with her baby days like he never got to be with Shirley Ann, because he was overseas so long. Connie had brown eyes and brown hair and was a plump, beautiful baby. We enjoyed her so much. She had brown eyes and brown hair like mine."

In those days, dryers were almost unheard of. The young family had a washing machine, but Miss Odell hung the clothes on an outside clothes line to dry. Today, we call that a solar dryer. The family became Miss Odell's family with a Collie dog, named Prince, who had a habit of straddling a corner of the chain link fence to jump outside. Prince would roam around, and then jump back in. Later, another Collie named Ginger joined the family. She had a litter of puppies, which were all sold but one.

"The girls loved them so much," says Miss Odell. "The one we kept was called Cindy. Shirley and Connie used to push her around in their doll buggy. They had lots of fun in that yard!

"We had such nice neighbors and the girls used to dress up in play clothes—women's hats and high heel shoes. They would practice and put on a show down at the Turner's house. There were four Turner girls. We had two girls; and there was Charlotte, who lived next door at the Smith's house. They would have such a good time putting on a play, singing and dancing around," continues Miss Odell. "Virginia Turner and I would be the audience and watch. For them, we'd bake cookies and always there was Kool-aid of all different colors and flavors. The children used to set up a little table in the front of our home and sell Kool-aid for one cent a glass and cookies. Of course, they'd eat and drink most of it—what a loosing proposition that would be! But we'd always think of the fun they had."

Miss Odell and Harold lived on Ashleman with their children, who walked to school one-half block to the LaVega grade school until Shirley was ready for High School.

*Odell Neel (graduation - 1937)*

# MISS ODELL, MY MOTHER

As of this writing, tomorrow would be Mom's and Dad's 69th wedding anniversary (August 9, 2011). Of course, Harold passed on about three years ago now. Mom may be joining Dad soon. Naturally, there is no way to tell when that moment will come. She seems so peaceful today. Yesterday, she asked when the 9th was. She was clear that Dad was coming for her.

She is the romantic to the end. She was always in love with my Dad. Even when no one else could see what she saw in him, he was her one and only true love.

Connie Dell (1) and Shirley Ann (6)

Shirley and I were fortunate to have such a mother. She was devoted to us. Her morals were very high. She was a Christian woman. On the other hand, she also taught us to be independent thinkers and strong women. There was never a question in my mind that I could do whatever I put my mind toward doing.

Dad wasn't quite as supportive of those ideas. He didn't want me to go to college and major in English and become a teacher. I wanted to major in English and become a writer. So...what I really did was get a one-year certificate in secretarial and accounting, which gave me the ability to work in almost every office in America. Eventually, I did enroll in Journalism classes. I wasn't able to continue with that at a local University, because I had young children, which made it challenging to get them off to school and to a class at 8 a.m. It was just plain too difficult to schedule, so I ended up in an online program in Small Business and Marketing. Just about everything ends up about marketing. Writing heavily relies on marketing. Isn't everything?

Shirley also had some starts and stops in her education. She began in home economics and realized that teaching was just not her thing. She was always so shy that standing up in front of a group would have just been too much for her. She changed her major to business. Then later, when her kids were still in school, she finally finished a degree in programming. Unfortunately, she wasn't able to do much in that field not because she was under-skilled, a woman, or anything else. It just seemed like the timing was off for her.

Mom taught us from little girls to be good homemakers. I'm not sure either of us were ever happy homemakers or even all that good at making a home the squeaky clean home that our mom kept. Maybe that was our rebellion.

We did learn to cook at a young age. By the time I was nine, I could bake chocolate chip cookies from scratch - you actually had to, the mixes weren't even available back then. We learned to do needlework, mostly embroidery, and sew. We had our cleaning chores to do, as well.

Mother spent quality time with us. I remember whole days devoted to craft projects. We had some interesting ones, such as the fake plant maker. It was green plastic goo and wire, I suppose. I thought it was amazing. It might not have been, because I was only about nine or 10 at the time.

When I was in the fifth grade, Mom and Dad bought into a franchise dress shop. Shirley and I would spend Saturdays with Mom working at the dress shop. We learned a lot, such as how to give change, how to talk to the customers, and how to decorate the windows to make them pretty.

There was little that Mom did that Shirley and I did not do. We spent more time with Mom than with Dad. We actually hated spending time with him most of the time. That's because his idea of having fun was to get a little drunk and take us fishing. I hated to fish. And I hated my dad when he was drinking. He became very obnoxious and insisted on lecturing us for hours and hours and hours. The two seemed to go together and was something to be avoided, as I recall.

Growing up in the 50s and 60s was so different to the environment that my own children were subjected to. People were just a bit more naïve in the 50s and 60s. I don't think Shirley had drugs in her school, but I did in mine - well, at least, alcohol. Marijuana didn't come up until the late 60s and 70s. I can't remember the first time I was offered pot. I also don't remember what I did about it, either. It seemed to be a trendy thing to smoke pot. Of course, I wasn't exactly the trendy person either. I did like the hippy style of clothing, I think. I didn't get too radical with it, because I also had to dress the part for work. Business dress then was a lot stricter: hose, skirt/dress, heels. Pantsuits had just become acceptable in some workplaces, but they were reserved for Friday's dress down day.

Mom was primarily a homemaker. I was not. Shirley adapted well to being a homemaker. I did not. I was on my second marriage and into my 30s when we adopted Sam. I quit my job at the telephone company to be more attractive for adoption. Being a mom was on my list of passions.

I really think this passion for motherhood came from Mom. She was a super mother. It was totally natural for her; and, it is my belief that she was born to be Shirley's and my mom. I'm not sure what our contributions to the world are so great that Mom would have that job. Or should I say, I don't know that I've done anything that remarkable with my life to deserve such a special mom. As a writer, I've written a lot of stuff, but has it been life altering? I don't think so! But then, sometimes we don't know what touches other people. Hopefully, this book is an important book for people who are experiencing similar situations.

As mom's health has declined, I've had to change my thinking. I used to think week-by-week with her. Now, it is day-by-day with her, and beginning to be more like hour-by-hour. Her health can change without a moment's notice. Yes, it is like riding a roller coaster to some degree. But I willingly signed onto this ride. I agreed to be here with my mom through whatever she had to go through. I agreed to be her support network and love her the way she had loved me when I was just a child.

In many ways, it is like having a child and trying to carve out life as a separate entity, while still being there when I feel it is required. No, she's not a child, but her needs are similar. When she has a problem, I'm the one who can help fix it. Sometimes she just needs me to listen. Sometimes I have to fix the television, the lamp or something as simple as replacing a light bulb. Sometimes I need to go shop for her. Sometimes I need to be the advocate for her when her voice might get lost or unnoticed. I'm the caregiver. I chose this job when I moved her from Tennessee to Massachusetts.

Hospice is one of the best things that I discovered. They are there for the last six months for end-of-life services, but that definition has been expanded a good deal. If the illness is expected not to get better and is life-threatening, then Hospice can come in, which means that they might be there for more than a year or even come and go if the situation improves. Mom didn't want to go to the hospital any more. They couldn't fix her and the hospital was so hard on her.

I've been fortunate to have had my mom here in the same town for about 10 months now. I've been able to be with her for some part of most days. We've talked, we've sewn or crocheted, and we've been together, which is the most important thing. I make sure that I don't have to do anything other than just be with my mom.

Perhaps, one of the hardest things I've done, was just telling her that I was married to a woman. My being homosexual after two marriages to men failed didn't seem odd to my mom at all. While she lived in Tennessee, I chose not to tell her. Although I think she may have suspected it, I did not want to make her life overly complicated by people who would have responded negatively to this idea.

Am I homosexual or bisexual? Well, to be truthful, I've never analyzed it. I just fell in love with my Joyce and I'd already decided not to be with men again. They're just too difficult for me and are not capable of showing their love in the way I need.

Mom not only accepted Joyce, she was delighted to have one more daughter. Mom's love has always been unconditional. She has treated Joyce as a daughter.

Mom, Connie, and Joyce

It's been difficult for Joyce with Mom's failing health, because Joyce, too, is experiencing some health issues. She has a hip that needs replacing and has suffered from Shingles for more than six weeks now. But she's been very supportive for whatever I've needed to do, including staying with mom until about 11 p.m. when I could get a sitter to come in.

My mom never fails to tell me that she loves me forever. I tell her the same. Today, as I'm writing I am also sitting in her room. She's breathing very slowly today, but she seems peaceful. It's also Mom and Dad's anniversary. They would have been married 69 years. Will this be the day? I cannot answer that. It is up to Mom. It would be a rather romantic ending, but it's hard to predict such things. I just want to keep her comfortable.

It's hard when her breathing gets raspy sounding, like she's struggling. But the morphine drops actually help with that. We've taken her off all medications with the exception of comfort meds, like the Atropine drops that dry up some of the extra secretions, the morphine that helps her breathing, and the Lorazapan keeps her calm. Sometimes her body just twitches all over, and that's when the Lorazapan can really help her.

As I'm sitting here watching over my mom, watching her sleep, she is so peaceful and beautiful. I'm still feeling the presence of *Light Beings* and *Angels*. I'm feeling quite peaceful, although I know it is just a matter of time. Will it be in the next hour or the next? I don't know, but I know I can be here with her. I cannot be with her 24/7, because that would be unhealthy for me, but fortunately I have some aides coming in through the night.

I know mere words are not adequate to describe the deep love and admiration that Shirley and I have for our mom. I know a lot of people who have sort of a love-hate relationship with their mom. I'm sorry for those people. Our mom was probably the sweetest mother on the planet. Oh, I may not have been a perfect child and there may have been some punishment dealt out along the way, but overall our mom was always there for us. We knew we were loved all our lives and as adults, as well.

Even as a grandmother, Mom was super. She would play dominoes with my kids. She even taught them how to count by fives, which is needed to play dominoes. She made cookies with them. She spent quality time with them, even though they didn't see her that often.

She did the same with Shirley's children, as well. But we didn't live in the same town as Mom and Dad, which certainly put a dent into grandmother time. When Shirley and I grew up, Mom's parents lived in the same town, which gave us ample time to spend with grandparents. Olivia and Sidney were excellent grandparents. We called them Mam-maw and Pap-paw.

Pap-paw built swings on either end of Mam-maw's clothesline. We made jellies with Mam-maw, especially Plum Jelly! Plums grew in the back yard along with squash, tomatoes, and black-eyed peas. While some folks have never even tasted black-eyed peas, they were among my favorite foods. I liked them fresh with snaps in them. Okra was the one thing my Mam-maw wouldn't eat, and I can't remember if their garden ever had any.

Mom grew okra. I loved it! She would cut it up, bread it, and fry it. I don't tend to cook this often, but I do love it! I also love eggplant, which is sliced thin, breaded and fried. As a truly Southern cook, just about anything can be breaded and fried. However, I do try to tone that down by doing more baking than frying. You can bread the veggies, but putting them in the oven makes them healthier.

Cooking was something Mom taught us. Dad taught Mom how to cook some things that he learned in the army or at the bakery. He had been head cook of an army hospital during WWII. But at our house, Mom was the primary cook. It was rare that Dad did any cooking.

I enjoy cooking and picked up a lot of recipes and ideas from Mom over the years. I never got into the bread baking like Mom. I'd like to, but that takes time. I sometimes buy bread loaves in a can or a box. I even bought a second-hand bread machine. I also tend to get the chocolate chip cookie dough that only requires you to break the squares up to cook. That's super lazy, I'm sure. However, you can't always make time to do all the cooking you want and still do any work.

When we would visit Mom in Tennessee, the thing I remember most was that Mom didn't eat much. She had a rather poor appetite. Shirley and I would go into Bolivar to the Wal-Mart and we would buy stuff that we knew Mom liked. She seemed to eat well when we made a good meal for her. One year, we bought avocados. You would have thought it was some delicacy! She loved eating them.

Although she did have a couple of ladies taking care of her, they weren't cooks. So, they bought a lot of frozen meals. These were probably not even good for her, because pre-packaged food tends to be high in sodium. Mom's congestive heart failure made her retain water. She was on diuretics or commonly known as water pills. But she was probably eating too much salt.

This was something we learned during her hospital stays in Massachusetts. Of course, I had a talk with the kitchen staff at the assisted living facility, but the truth was that they tried to cook with no salt. They had a lot of residents who had heart issues. They could help Mom make smarter decisions about her food, but they couldn't keep her from eating anything. I assured them that any help in eating low sodium was helping.

It is often the small things that matter to Mom. She could give up salt, but she wanted something in its place. The hospital told her that the salt replacement was still higher in sodium than they would like her to have. I bought her lemon pepper. She carries it to every meal. Her purse is filled with tissues and lemon pepper.

Mom loves going down to meals, because she eats with friends. The assisted living is "living in luxury,'" she says. Mom doesn't have to clean; the facility does that along with changing her bed every week and washing the bedding. Mom washes her own clothes. But when Hospice came in, she needed to let go of that. She did. She also needed assistance taking showers. She isn't the easiest person to help. She still got up and took her own shower, when the mood struck her.

At the point we brought in Hospice, Mom had gotten a little worse. She couldn't bend over to put on her shoes. She couldn't walk down stairs, because she would get so out of breath. If she did walk downstairs – walk to the elevator and go down - by the time she got down to a meal, she was so winded that she couldn't eat.

Mom is still hard to take care of some days. She wants to remain independent. At the same time, she really needs help most of the time with the small stuff like putting on shoes. Some days, she just gets impatient and puts her own shoes on. I try to be there at that point in the late afternoon, so I can help. Mom, however, doesn't want to go down to eat if I'm there. She'd prefer to visit. She says that she isn't hungry. I think she's gotten used to eating three meals!

I encourage her. I try not to hover or be overly fussy, but her breathing seems to be harder lately. I worry that she's filling up with fluids again. This would mean the cycle would repeat. Lasix to get rid of the fluid would be given. The Lasix tends to irritate her urinary tract and make it swell, which means that it backs up and becomes infected. They'll give her antibiotics, which hopefully doesn't have side effects. Some of them have been so strong that they upset her entire gastric system.

Odell Neel Jones in her assisted living apartment.

# MISS ODELL'S ELDER CARE

My mom and dad retired early. They had lived in Texas for all of our growing up years. Dad got transferred first to Little Rock, AR, then Memphis, TN. At 55, he was offered a retirement package that was impossible to refuse. They chose to retire in rural Tennessee in a small retirement community around a lake. It was ideal for them. They went fishing, camping, and traveling. They enjoyed their retirement years. There came a time, however, that they began to have health issues. Unfortunately, by that time, it was too difficult for them to even consider moving.

Shirley and I became aware of their health issues along with demands to come take care of Mom. She had fallen at the Kroger, a grocery store a town or so away. She was taken into Jackson, TN, to the hospital there. She had hip surgery, but Dad is the one that really needed help. He couldn't see. He couldn't drive into Jackson to see Mom. He couldn't even feed himself, because he couldn't navigate the kitchen. Mom took care of all of this.

Shirley had to go. She stayed a month. I had a job at a church in Massachusetts at this point, and I really couldn't take off. Shirley was retired. Not even six months later, Mom fell at home and broke her other hip. Shirley again had to go and stay about a month to take care of Dad and be there for Mom.

They seemed to still be fairly independent, although Mom was on a walker. She began driving most of the time, because Dad's eyesight was so bad. I stopped by to see them on my way to or from Texas for my once a year drive back to Denton, TX. I wasn't there long, but Shirley had given me the heads up: someone needed to take them into Jackson to get their hearing aids cleaned.

I did that and also got them a new microwave for which Sears would install. That was a good get, since Mom's had worn out. She used hers a lot, so it was good to get her a new one. They really had a hard time standing for the length of time needed to get the transaction to go through. I finally found a chair for one of them. Dad insisted Mom sit, but I thought he was in more need of sitting than she was.

I tried to find another, but Dad just wanted me to hurry with the sale. I did. I worried about them, but Mom kept assuring me they were okay. They took care of each other.

Mom was the only driver at some point, because Dad couldn't even see shapes or the road. I'm not exactly sure when he decided that he wasn't safe. Shirley and I knew he wasn't safe years before he stopped driving. Mom was a competent driver. She had taught me to drive when I was a teenager. But there was a time when they were both in the car and had just gone to the bank, and then Mom was going to drive them home. Dad yelled at Mom that she was turning the wrong way. She wasn't, but he upset her to the point that she got confused. Instead of pressing the brakes, she pressed the gas pedal. They went sailing across the street and the gully and ended up rolling the car.

The car wasn't totaled, but they both ended up with bumps and bruises. This was the beginning of a downward spiral for them.

Again, Shirley got the call to come take care of them. She did. Dad was having a lot of trouble and pain related more to his intestines than related directly to the car accident. He needed a lot of care. Shirley and Mom looked into assisted living. Dad was too ill for assisted living. They looked into nursing home care. Mom was not ill enough for that. So, they looked into rehab for Dad. After rehab, he could come home with home care.

Shirley couldn't stay and take care of them, but she did arrange for care with a service that offered aides. They could even take Mom to the grocery store or any other place. There was an additional cost. Mother said they could afford it.

Not long after Shirley was home, Mom wanted to change everything. She fired the service and hired the women privately. There were some women that she hired from references from the other women.

Unfortunately, even though there was 24/7 care coverage, Dad wanted Mom to take care of him. At this point he was in adult diapers and unable to control any of these functions. This sort of stress on Mom caused her to go to the hospital. They diagnosed her as having congestive heart failure. She returned home with oxygen, and the ladies needed to care for them both. Mother was still very independent, but Dad required 24/7.

Shirley found out that Dad's hospital bed was in Mom's and Dad's bedroom. She had the aides move it before Mom returned home.

This is the way it was for a couple of years before Dad passed. After Harold died in September, 2008, Miss Odell wanted to stay in their home in Tennessee. She didn't want Shirley or I to make her move where we were.

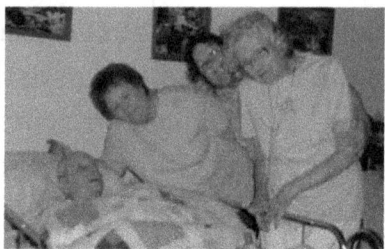

Dad, Shirley, Connie, Mom
April (2008)

There really wasn't even any question in my mind about where she would go; she would go to California. She thought Massachusetts was the US version of Siberia. But that isn't the way it happened!

Mom had 24 hour care for Dad, but once he was gone, the money wasn't there. Not only did the Social Security get cut but the annuity that they had lived on had also expired with his death. So, she cut back to two ladies and didn't have anyone at night, which made both Shirley and I a bit worried. Then, one of the ladies moved in. It probably wasn't quite that quick, but it felt that way.

Mother's money began to disappear. The bank called Shirley, and she called me. We tried to take over the bills, but Mother was very resistant. We went to visit in April. Mother and the health aide whom we'll call Nancy to protect her identity agreed to stop investing in sweepstakes. Mother was still convinced that 2 million dollars was on its way to her.

We were only there a few days, and then we returned to our homes and our lives. Mother, however, continued investing in sweepstakes. By the end of August, we knew we were going to have to do something drastic. I had taken over the money at that point, because Shirley had made herself ill trying to work with Mom. She also found herself yelling at Mother. We had never yelled at our mother!

I was steadfast as I could be, but I was concerned that she would not have access to any money and live in rural Tennessee. The bank closed her bank account, because Nancy decided to be Shirley or I and try to withdraw money. Thank goodness, she was stopped. Our mother, however, was very disturbed and confused. It was hard to tell if she was suffering from dementia or if Nancy was hurting her or just what was going on. She just couldn't understand that if I put $2,000 into her account for paying bills and buying groceries, and she sent it off to a sweepstakes that that money was gone.

In October of that same year (2010), Shirley and I met in Memphis, TN. We didn't tell Mom we were coming, because we didn't want Nancy to hurt her or do something rash. Our surprise visit was met with some confusion. We had a nice conversation with Mom that first night and she agreed to go to Massachusetts with me. Shirley and her husband, Jerry, weren't sure what their plans were long-term. He had just retired. We knew Mom couldn't move twice, so we made arrangements to move her to Massachusetts with me.

Before going to Tennessee, a lot of other work had to be done. I had to find a place for Mom to live, put down money to reserve it. To learn more about this story, see *How to Find Appropriate Housing*.

It was my job to try to coordinate the timing of things and work out all the logistics for mother's move on my end. I'm not sure how I managed to get it all to work as easy as I did. I arranged for her to move into an assisted living facility in Franklin, MA, where I live. I thought it would take a bit to get furniture here, but the mover made it almost as fast as we did flying.

Flying with Mom and her oxygen is another story. See *How to Move an Elder* for that story.

In Rural Tennessee, there isn't what I would call stellar medical care. While it was available in Memphis, that was about an hour away. Jackson, TN, was also about 45 minutes away, and provided my parents with specialty care. But even after having hip surgery, my mom was followed by her primary care doctor in Bolivar, TN. They didn't actually live in Bolivar. They lived in a rural area around a man-made lake in what was meant to be a retirement community. However, it lacked all the services retirees need, such as ambulance service, a grocery store, snow and ice removal for the roads, and many other services that make elders lives livable in their family home.

The first thing that I did after getting Mom settled into her new space was to get her into the doctor and get checked out. She really seemed pretty okay at that time: maybe even more than okay. I felt that she was stronger only a week or so after getting her to Massachusetts. There were challenges, of course. For example, the dining room was downstairs. The assisted living facility had elevators, so the stairs part wasn't an issue. But where my mom's apartment was located, she had to walk down two hallways. One hallway was very long; the other was somewhat more doable. Mom's walker actually made this walk more challenging. She was picking it up and putting it down, because it didn't slide or roll.

There were a couple of reasons that I felt Mom was doing better so soon. First of all, she slept well. Second of all, no one was making her get dressed and go in the car to get money. That was what Nancy seemed to do each day. More and more and more money was flying out of mom's account. She was not being honest with us about what was happening, which was so unlike our mom on several levels. I think that also caused Mom a lot of stress, which she no longer had in her own apartment.

Mom and Dad were frugal people. From the depression days forward, mother learned how to conserve, reuse, and recycle. She had been doing it all her life. Beginning with childhood, clothing was made from the best materials, which would be wrapped around the ground up wheat (flour). These sacks were good cotton and could be sewn into just about everything from dresses to bloomers.

Each year at holiday time, I sent mom Pandolfi's Chocolate Fudge. After the candy is gone, Mother uses the box to store pens and pencils in. It's really cute how she manages to recycle just about anything.

Left: Connie, Shirley, and Miss Odell making chocolate meringue pie at Miss Odell's Tennessee home.

# HOW TO NAVIGATE THE FINANCES

Finances are always a difficult subject to broach, especially, when the money isn't yours. There are times when you have no choice but to cross that money bridge. When you love someone and care about their welfare, the financial stability of your loved one is part of that care.

In January, 2010, our frugal mom wrote a $10,000 check to an individual for whom we had no idea who they were. That wouldn't have been so bad, but there were two more such checks. Only one was caught by the bank. Money began flying out of our mother's account at a very fast clip. We would never have known about it, if the bank had not called my sister, Shirley, who at that point held the Power of Attorney.

Naturally, we talked. We worried. We asked what was going on. For the first time in our whole lives, Mom lied to us. She'd been scammed, but she didn't believe it. She believed that two million dollars were going to be delivered to her door. But the money to scams didn't stop, it just kept going and going. She'd take out one or two thousand dollars a day.

For the most part, Shirley was dealing with this. She tried to take over the paying of bills, but Mother was fighting her. She and Nancy (not the actual name of the health aide that was part of the scam) presented a united front, but one that was so flimsy that we knew what was going on. In truth, Nancy was leading the way for all the money going to sweepstakes and scams.

We visited in April, as we had several years in a row. Nancy was fully ensconced at the house, but Mom and Nancy claimed it was temporary. They both promised the sweepstakes were a thing of the past. It didn't stop. It just kept on going. Shirley got tricked into giving the finances back, then had to take it over again. At some point, I stepped in. Shirley's blood pressure shot sky high from the stress of dealing with Mom and her money. The bank wanted to close Mom's accounts. That upset me, because she was living in rural Tennessee and not having access to any money seemed scary to me.

The bank said they felt Mom was being elder abused and that they had no other choice but to close the accounts. I set up accounts and received the money, but I could see we had bigger issues. I wasn't sure if Nancy would hurt Mom, but Mom was making me think she was losing her mind. She was always the most frugal woman on the planet and this crazy sweepstakes stuff was just too strange to be coming from our mom.

I had pretty much gotten in control of the money and had been working to get all of Mom's bills sent to me and on an automatic schedule for online bill paying. That's what made it work in my life. But we still had the issue that Mom was in rural Tennessee and had no bank account and no access to money.

Fortunately, we had already made a lot of plans. We were going to go to Tennessee and move Mom to Franklin, MA, where I lived. It sounded simple, but Mom was on oxygen and couldn't walk long distances. Just the oxygen was a huge challenge, but one that was resolved easily. I found a company called Oxygen-to-go, which for a fee would send you a crate with a portable oxygen concentrator. You simply chose the number of batteries that you needed. We had a straight thru flight, so three hours was adequate.

Best laid plans and all of that! The airline canceled the non-stop flight and moved us to a little later flight. This flight stopped over in New York City. We didn't have to change planes, which made things a little less complicated, but we still had to leave the plane. I needed to charge the battery to make it to Boston.

We made it to Boston without a problem. But it was getting anywhere else, such as to our motel, which was going to be a problem. Fortunately, Mom could go without her oxygen for short periods, especially if she was at rest. Riding to our motel seemed to work.

I'm getting ahead of myself. First, Shirley and I had to get to Tennessee! Shirley and I met in Memphis at the airport and headed out to Bolivar. We spent the night in Bolivar.

We visited the banks and set things straight there. We drove out to Mom's, but no one was home. We waited down the street and watched them pull into the driveway. We weren't sure what sort of entrance we should make. Nancy greeted us with a cell phone attached to her head telling someone her sisters were here. Maybe we weren't supposed to hear that or maybe she was hopeful that she rated as such. She didn't!

One of the reasons the bank was closing Mom's accounts was that Nancy tried passing herself off as Shirley or I at the bank trying to remove money from Mom's account. I was hoping that the bank would prosecute. They did not. Instead, they just closed the account and therefore closed their responsibility.

We did try to get Nancy investigated and have her arrested, but we simply did not have enough proof. It was hard to tell if Nancy had truly been doing this to Mom or if they were somewhat united in their sweepstakes entry addiction. What proof did we have?

At this point, I was ready to whisk Mom up to Massachusetts and forget about everything else. I just wanted to protect Mom and get her to a place where she could be fully who she was with people her own age and interests. Mom was always a social person and had been isolated in rural Tennessee for much too long.

Now that all the worries about her money are mostly in the past, it's easier to think about how we might have gone about it differently. First, I think when our dad passed, we needed to have been more involved in helping Mom figure out what she could and could not afford. Instead, we were pretty hands off. We helped her get all of her affairs in order, but we didn't go to the next step, which would have been to see what was coming in and what was going out. Then, we could have helped Mom be comfortable with the smaller income that she was getting.

Mom never intended to throw away her money, but she was trying to invest in sweepstakes to gain more money to take care of her perceived shortfall. She was misguided, of course. And Nancy certainly wasn't helping matters. You see, Nancy believed that the money was a given. She also had a personal relationship with the chief scammer.

Mom's telephone bill was $400 to $800 a month. This was the same Mother, who refused to let Shirley or I pay for Touch-Tone Service so that we could get on the Internet when we visited. Touch-Tone Service was something like $2.50 a month just to give you perspective on money.

When looking into the finances of your elder, you should know what and how much money is in Certificate of Deposits, Money Market Accounts, and what is invested in the stock market or other investments. One way to take the focus off of the delicate nature of snooping to find out about your elder's finances is to suggest that you accompany them to a meeting with a financial planner. The financial planner can be objective about the money and offer suggestions to move money around to make it most useful for your elder.

As you get older, money invested in riskier financial markets should be moved into safe alternatives. And sweepstakes are not investments. They are more like gambling without having the right cards!

Another option for elders is to plan for aging in place, which includes planning for different levels of care they might need and preparing for the amount of money they will need to acquire those services. Senior living insurance or long-term insurance has become a popular way to plan. However, if you have any medical issues, you may not qualify for the insurance plan.

One of the greatest needs is for daily money management, according to AARP. In 1981, a free money-management system was developed by AARP, including volunteers, system safeguards, monthly reporting, and third-party oversight. In 1991, Mass Home Care, had about 30 non-profit agencies start a similar program. It has expanded to cover approximately 1200 clients per month and is the largest such service in America.

Part of the issue with finances is also legal. A Power of Attorney gives you the legal capacity to act for your loved one. Without a Power of Attorney, the bank should not discuss banking matters. To safeguard your loved one, having the legal papers in place is the best first step. Putting other people's names on your account can feel risky to a senior, so begin with a Will, Power of Attorney, and Health Care Proxy. This will be a conversation you need to have well before any need for financial intervention occurs. While some people naturally think about Estate Planning, others don't feel they have enough money or assets to warrant this. That is simply not the case. Everyone needs these legal papers.

According to nolo.com, taking over only the part of the finances for which your elder is having difficulty will allow your elder their dignity. Taking over of an elder's finances can be just as overwhelming for you, especially if they have been badly neglected.

There is some important information to gather to help you gain better control of the financial aspect of your elder. The following list includes common information that you will likely be asked to gather at numerous points along your journey with your elder.

- All insurance polices including health, disability, and policies related to short or long term care.
- Social security numbers and dates of birth.
- Important cards such as Medicare or in some instances Medicaid.
- A good list of medical needs including health conditions and both prescribed and over the counter medications utilized.
- Copies of loans and mortgages.
- Copies of investment papers including real estate, retirement plans, dividends, stocks, bonds, and any other financial information related to investments such as titles to owned vehicles.
- Bank accounts.
- Income sources and amounts.
- Monthly living expense requirements as well as annual items such as property taxes or association fees.
- Tax returns, safe deposit boxes and keys, keys to vehicles and homes.
- A list of all pertinent doctors, lawyers, and insurance brokers.
- Pet information; especially vet information as well as your parent's desires upon an illness or death of a loved pet; or in case of your elder's death, who is bequeathed the pet?
- Funeral and burial wishes including burial plots.
- Copies of living wills.
SOURCE: Brighthub.com

Shirley (7) and Connie (2)

Connie and Shirley (1996)

Shirley and Connie (2008)

Connie, Mom, Shirley (2009)

# KEEPING FAMILY TUNED-IN

One of the most important parts of being my mother's caregiver was to take on keeping the rest of the family informed. I took on that job seriously and willingly. I only have one sibling: my sister, Shirley. We each live on opposite coasts. We both love our mother deeply, and we love each other, as well.

This is our family. But it is probably not much different to yours. You may have more siblings; thus, more love. Make no mistake, whether you agreed to keeping them informed, it comes with the job!

Communication is always the backbone of holding any family together. When a parent or other loved one enters an assisted living facility, rehab center, or nursing home, they need an advocate and a supporting family member. They need someone they can count on to take care of whatever it is that they can no longer do themselves. They need someone to take them to doctors' visits and be a listening ear for them. They need someone to help them remember what they need to discuss with their doctor, and what the doctor tells them.

Assisted living facilities often have vans or buses that they use to take residents on field trips and for doctor's appointments. However, you may find, like I did, that their bus wasn't useable by my mom. She could not have stepped up into the bus. Even with help that would have been hazardous.

There are often other services available through the local council on aging or senior center. For example, in Franklin, MA, there is a volunteer network of drivers, who will take a senior to a doctor's appointment. If you need to be an advocate for your senior, however, this would be the opportunity to step up to that plate by driving and being that second pair of ears.

The other part of the communication package is keeping the rest of the family informed about the loved one you have in common. It is not necessary to report every detail of every day. That would just be overkill, but significant issues do need to be reported.

Each of the times my mom went into the hospital was a significant issue to report. Keeping my sister informed about the health of our mother was my responsibility. Just because she lives on the opposite coast from me should not mean that surprises about our mom's health should blindside her. Naturally, I'm the one that sits in the Emergency Room with our mom. I'm the one that loses sleep on those nights waiting for the hospital to do what they do to admit her. If the circumstances had been different, Shirley would be the one to keep me informed.

My sister relies on me to let her know about our mother. It would be easy to slip into being a martyr and think about all the ways that caring for our mom has impacted my life. It is imperative to rise above that. Your loved one needs you. You chose the job of caregiver and this is what that means. It's like having a child. You can't decide that you don't want the responsibility when it suddenly gets a little difficult! Nor can you abdicate your responsibility for your loved one.

Mom is always apologetic about having to go to the Emergency Room (ER). She knows it is hard on me, but I always know it is harder on her. I stay with her, because she often ends up at the hospital without her hearing aids, which greatly diminishes communication between her and the medical staff. In fact, the nursing staff at her assisted living facility encourages her to leave hearing aids behind, because they have had residents go to the hospital and lose them. They may be small, but they cost a lot!

Hospitals are hard places for sick people to be, which I know is rather ironic, since sick people go to hospitals to get better. The problem is the slowness at which hospitals operate. I'm sure they do their best. I'm not complaining about anything specific. When you arrive at a hospital, you get looked at by a triage nurse. If you come in by ambulance, you usually get put into a room quicker. From there, nothing happens very quickly.

Even when you see a doctor and get a diagnoses, prognosis, and determine that they're going to admit you, then time really stands still. One of our visits brought Mom in about 3 p.m., but she wasn't settled into a room until about 2 a.m. The problem is that until she is settled into a room, she can't truly relax and sleep. To be truthful, she can't even get that much relaxation and sleep anyplace in the hospital. It's harder to sleep in the ER, because there is always noise. They also don't have nurse buttons to call for help in all places in the ER. For this reason, I just never felt it reasonable to leave Mom alone in the ER. I didn't race off to the hospital either! I usually gave it an hour or two. In that way, I could finish up what I needed to finish in my work day, but still be there for Mom.

The hospital was limited in what they could do for Mom. They could stabilize her and admit her while they treated her. After several trips to the hospital, Mom simply didn't want to go back. It always took her so long to recover from being in the hospital that the hospital stays seemingly ran together. That's when I had a talk with the nursing staff at the assisted living facility. They suggested that I get Hospice on board.

Hospice works quickly. They came in, ordered a wheel chair, a hospital bed and a portable commode for Mom's room. They arranged for an aide to come in to assist with her shower two times a week. Mom couldn't put her shoes on any more, because when she bent over she would get too out of breath. The assisted living aides began assisting her with that. We arranged for the laundry to be done by the assisted living facility. Then, there was the issue of putting the laundry away. We arranged for that, as well. Hospice was fantastic!

Getting Hospice on board was another rather large decision that needed to be shared with my sister. The fact is that Mom had congestive heart failure. Three out of the four heart valves were leaking and they couldn't do surgery on her, because she wouldn't make it through the surgery. There was no fix for Mom. This was what it was!

It was a matter of time. Mom's heart was a ticking bomb, and it was evident that Mom was going through cycles that were very hard on her body. She would take on fluid, Lasix would be prescribed, the Lasix irritated her urinary tract and caused it to swell and back up, which then caused an infection in her bladder. She'd go on some heavy duty antibiotic, which caused nausea and diarrhea. She'd finally get over that cycle for a few days or week or more, and then it would start all over again.

Here's where it becomes super important to communicate with your family. Mom had a time bomb that could go off at any time. Not to tell Shirley about this would have been like lying. This was major! Mom wanted Shirley to come. Mom knew it was only a matter of time for her. She was ready, but she wanted to see Shirley first.

I had to do a lot of talking to get Shirley to understand that she needed to come. It came at a bad time for her. She and her husband had decided to buy a new home. They would be moving into their home when it would be best for them to come. Stacie, my niece, and her family also bought a new home and would be moving into their home about the same time. Not being here and seeing how Mom was when she was sick was an issue of communication that I had to navigate.

It wasn't that I was unconvincing, but there was a distinct resistance due to moving plans. Shirley understood that if she didn't come, Mom might not be here later in the year when it was a better time for her.

Left Back: Connie (Rusty, the Chihuahua in arms), Shirley, Sarah (11), Stacie (Shirley's daughter)
Left Front: Erin (Connie's daughter), Miss Odell, Tyler (8)

As it turns out, Shirley and Stacie picked a date in July, 2011. Stacie brought along her husband, Mark, and their two children, Sarah and Tyler. My youngest daughter, Erin, also came. It was a very nice week for Mom. She loved being with everyone.

Then, after everyone left, she got sick again. I communicated that to Shirley. It was my responsibility to let her know how her illness was affecting her. When Mom took a turn for the worst, it wasn't an easy call to make. Then, she rallied, and I communicated that.

It was important to prepare Shirley for what I was afraid was our mom's final days. How would she take it, if she had been here, seen Mom, and thought, "Oh, she's just doing great!" Then, I call her to tell her Mom passed. How would my sister react? How would she be able to process that? It was my job to help my sister understand what was happening to our mom.

Mom had told me that she was ready more than once or twice. I knew Mom was very tired, and I wasn't sure she could fight this episode off. Shirley took the news hard. She just couldn't accept that news, and yet, I had to communicate it. She didn't want our precious mom to be gone from our lives. Because no matter how prepared you are for the death of your mom or dad or other important loved one in your life, you are never really ready! You keep hoping for a different solution.

Unfortunately, you cannot pick the time and place of your own death or that of anyone else. We don't know how the Universe of Energy really operates on a universal scale. We get glimpses into that world.

Some people are more sensitive to energy and can see more of it than others. But even though these people can see into that Universe of Energy, they, too, cannot know all. We live in the shadow of mystery. There are probably many psychological reasons that cause us to not consciously choose to know the mystery surrounding our death, even if we had the means to know.

There are plenty of people who know they are dying, but they still don't know when that will come. As long as we don't know, we can hold on to hope. That hope gives us the strength to live and to die.

It is sometimes harder for the survivors to deal with death, because we face the finality of our own life. Some of us are so afraid that we are paralyzed by the thought.

When you take on the responsibility of being the caregiver for your mom or dad or aunt or uncle or other loved one, you take on the responsibility for much more. Your responsibility extends out to the rest of the family. Those who are not giving care do not see what you see. They don't hear what you hear. They aren't in the loop like you are. That's the reason that communication is so important.

Just because the rest of the family is not taking on the responsibility for care giving to your loved one does not mean that the rest of the family cares less. It simply means that they don't see what you see on a daily basis, which is why you need to communicate often with the rest of the family, so they, too, can get the picture of what is going on with their loved one.

Perhaps, your situation is different and there are more caregivers. Great! But each caregiver does take on the responsibility of informing other family members. So if there are more caregivers, you need to communicate with the other caregivers and decide how the communication to other family can be handled.

One easy method of capturing what happens during a block of time when you are the caregiver is to write in a journal. Each caregiver can write down what medications were administered, what observations that they noticed. The end result is that the journal helps keep track of everything.

It can be made available in the room for the next caregiver. In this way, communication is then shared among those who are giving care. This is a tip that I have borrowed from Hospice and a local group of aides: Circle of Care. I found the journal entries to be helpful.

Naturally, there are many ways of communicating. However, the written communication journal provides continuity and flexibility at the same time. While telling the next caregiver helps, it is even better to be able to look back in the journal to see what has transpired over a period of time.

In lieu of a journal, a form can be used. Forms, however, do have some limits in that you may not think of every possibility on your form. That might mean some activity might not be recorded.

On the following pages is a sample form. The first form is blank ready to be used. The second form is filled out as a sample of how it might be used.

# CAREGIVER'S COMMUNICATION FORM

Date: _____
   Caregiver: _____

| Medication/Medical Equipment/Personal Care | Time Given/ When Used | Needs Assistance | Notes |
|---|---|---|---|
| | | | |
| | | | |
| | | | |
| | | | |
| | | | |
| | | | |
| | | | |
| | | | |
| | | | |
| | | | |
| | | | |
| | | | |
| | | | |
| | | | |
| | | | |
| | | | |
| | | | |
| | | | |
| | | | |
| | | | |

# CAREGIVER'S COMMUNICATION FORM

Date: 08-01-2011     Caregiver: Connie

| Medication/Medical Equipment/Personal Care | Time Given/When Used | Needs Assistance | Notes |
|---|---|---|---|
| Morphine – 2.5 ml | 8 p.m. | | Gave to help with breathing |
| Wanted to Get Up to Pee | 10 p.m. | Yes – takes 2 people | Called in Assisted Living Aide |
| Hearing Aids | | Thought lost hearing aids | Told her that they were safe in their container |
| Slept Peacefully | | | Left at 11 p.m. |
| | | | |
| | | | |
| | | | |
| | | | |

Left: Shirley, Mom, and Connie
in Miss Odell's home in Tennessee

# HOW TO MOVE AN ELDER

It is never ideal to move an elder, but there are times that it is necessary. When Shirley and I decided that we needed to move Mom, it wasn't a light decision. Mom was on oxygen and was too frail to be walking around the airport.

I wasn't sure if we could really fly Mom with her being on oxygen. However, I have a friend of a friend on oxygen and she flew to Florida, I believe. That helped me begin to think about transporting Mom.

I got online and found a company named Oxygen-to-go. They arrange portable oxygen concentrators for airline flights. That was the first step in realizing that I could move my mom.

Shirley and I did discuss whether or not such a move would kill our mom. That was certainly not our goal. We weighed the issues. At the rate things were going in rural Tennessee, we weren't sure Mom was going to survive anyway. Nancy kept getting Mom out in the car, so that she could get Mom to pull out money from the bank. We thought about just firing Nancy (not her real name), but we also figured that it wouldn't get rid of her. We began to believe that she was after Mom's car and house. And we weren't too far off! We explored the idea of an assisted living facility in Tennessee, but we knew that was still going to leave Mom alone in Tennessee. That was unacceptable!

With all that I knew about assisted living, nursing homes, and rehab centers, I knew that you really don't want to just leave a loved one at these facilities and go off and live your life. While assisted living offers a wide array of services, including taking residents to doctor's appointments, there are still different needs that require someone to be close by to assist the elder. For example, Mom cannot even get on the bus used by the assisted living facility where she lives. There was a large step up into the bus, which she would not have been able to negotiate.

I take Mom to all her doctors' appointments, do all her shopping, and pick up prescriptions. If I wasn't available to do that, I'm not sure assisted living would work for her.

But I'm getting ahead of myself, travel from Saulsbury, TN, to Franklin, MA, was going to be challenging. I began looking at prices of tickets and how to get the oxygen. Naturally, we were going to have to convince her to come to Massachusetts with me. She did agree, and it seemed she was ready for a change, as Mom kept saying: "I'm turning over a new leaf!"

Travel is not easy anymore. I had gone with a major airline and through a travel agent to get the desired return home with Mom: a nonstop from Memphis to Boston. I usually don't go to Boston, since Providence, RI, is about 45 minutes away and Boston is more like an hour to hour-and-a-half. But for a direct flight, it seemed the most doable.

I arranged for the oxygen based on the direct flight. The oxygen arrived in a huge blue crate in Tennessee. I spent some time reading directions to make sure that I knew how it operated. We went into Memphis the evening before our flights: Shirley back to Pleasanton, CA; Mom and I to Boston, MA. Joyce would pick us up in Boston.

We got into our motel room. I was feeling pretty good about everything. Mom had put the house up on the market; we had arranged for all of what Mom wanted to take with her to be picked up and transported to MA. All of the plans were working! Well, that is until I got the call from the airline canceling our direct flight.

Instead of it taking a mere three hours to get to MA, it was going to take the whole day. I knew we were in trouble, because I didn't have enough battery power for the oxygen generator to last all day. So I would have to plug that thing in every chance I got. This was not an easy task. You don't just plug it in on the plane and be done! We had to disembark, find an electrical outlet, and park Mom there.

We had a stop over in New York City. The airport was very crowded, but we did find a power outlet to recharge one of the batteries. Naturally, nothing was easy. Mom really needed to go to the potty, but I also needed her batteries to charge, which wasn't going to happen if we went off to the bathroom. I also knew that food was needed, but none of these things were going to work together easily. I didn't want to leave Mom by herself.

We ended up getting back on the plane. Mom went to the bathroom on the plane with me standing outside holding onto her oxygen. The stewardess found a banana for Mom and I to share. It hit the spot! So we were on our last leg of the journey.

It was very cold in Massachusetts; it was October. I managed to get all our luggage and the big blue crate, plus Mom all lined up at the curb for Joyce to pick us up. I had to dig out some warmer things for Mom. She needed gloves on her hands and an extra layer of clothing. I got her bundled and Joyce was finally able to get up to the terminal. The oxygen concentrator ran out of battery power shortly after we got in the car. I tried hooking it up to the cigarette lighter, but it wasn't working very well.

Fortunately, Mom was okay without the oxygen, because she was resting easy. Mom, however, was so tired. We went straight to the motel. I got Mom pretty much tucked in with the exception of food. So I sent Joyce to TGI Fridays for two plates of my favorite dish: parmesan crusted chicken and a side of three-cheese tortellini (they discontinued this menu item in 2011).

Mom didn't eat a lot, but she ate some. She was just so tired; it was hard for her to do anything. Luckily, we didn't need to do anything! We just needed to sleep. I didn't have any problems sleeping, either. I was pretty well wiped out.

The next morning, we arrived at Mom's new home: Forge Hill Senior Living. She loved it. They had fixed up a bed in her room, which was handy because she was so tired. I put her into the bed.

The long and short of it all: she survived the move. Her furniture and boxes arrived. We worked on a lot of it, but I simply got over-tired and had to stop for the day. I had the guys take the rest of the stuff to our house and it got dumped into my basement office.

It took awhile to get all the boxes unloaded and put away or taken to Goodwill. I still had some stuff to send Shirley. It took months for me to get it all over and put away.

Can you move an elder? Yes. But if they are on oxygen, over-estimate your need for battery power. Remember that airports are zoos. Get your elder a wheel chair, even if they think they can walk. The wheel chair comes with a personal transport, which then allows you to manage your own carry-ons.

Traveling with an elderly parent or other relative is very much like traveling with a child without the need to entertain. Make sure to take them to the restroom before boarding an airplane. While they can use the facilities on the plane, the tight quarters make it impossible to assist them.

Before you move, what needs to get done? Well, almost everything! First, you need to find the place where you want them to live. I felt strongly about keeping my mom as close as possible. Since I was moving her over a thousand miles, I wanted to make sure visiting her daily was a possibility. I moved her into an assisted living facility that was only five minutes from my home.

Ideally, you can take your elder to see the facility. Most facilities have an open house during the weekend, such as Sunday afternoon. This allows your senior to visit with residents and staff, possibly have a meal in the dining room, and check out the apartments.

Most assisted living facilities have different size apartments, such as efficiency (one room), one bedroom (includes a bedroom separate to living space), and two bedroom (ideal for a roommate or an elder who cannot part with her furniture). Naturally, the costs depend on the size of the apartment. Therefore, I arranged for mom to go into the efficiency apartment.

I signed the lease, because at that point, I had control of all the money. I wrote a check to reserve the apartment. In our case, we hadn't had the talk with our mom yet. I was a little hesitant to make all the arrangements; however, they needed to be in place before I brought Mom home with me.

Having the discussion with your elder about moving is a huge step. It's great if you can have mini-discussions over a longer period of time, but that might not be possible. Talk around nursing homes, assisted living facilities, or even moving in with you should come as early as possible. Shirley and I had a previous discussion about these issues between us and with our mom. That helps!

These are scary topics to elders. They don't want to give up their independence. They may need to give up their independence, but it doesn't mean they are going to be agreeable or willing.

Approaching the subject from the point of view of your own concern is the best way to open the discussion. Avoid saying things like, "Dad, we've decided it's time for you to go into a nursing home." That seems so final and robs your elder of buying into the process. Instead, if you show your genuine concern for their health and safety, then follow that by asking to be their advocate, there is a larger chance that your elder can see that you are helping them.

For example, you could say, "Mom, I'm concerned about you living alone way out here in the middle of nowhere. I'd feel better if you were close to me so I could check on you every day."

Any time you can begin the conversation with genuine concern for your senior's well-being, this is a plus. It is even better; if you can help facilitate a conversation that ends with the senior deciding that moving is a good idea.

Handling the resistant senior must be done in a compassionate manner. Find out to what they are resisting. Ask them to indulge you by visiting an assisted living facility with you. This might change their mind. In our case, Mom made the decision easily. Perhaps, she had just gotten worn down by the finance issues. Maybe she needed us to intervene. Maybe she liked it that we came unannounced to rescue her from what we perceived as a bad situation. We'll never know what her thought process was on the day she decided to move to Massachusetts with me. The fact was that she agreed.

In fact, she was quite cute! She agreed to move and then, in the middle of the night, she was up gathering stuff together to take with her. The very next day, she decided not only to move, but to put the house up on the market. This was a step, Shirley and I felt we could do later because we didn't think she would want to sell it. In fact, we thought she might want the possibility of returning there, if the assisted living facility turned out all wrong for her.

Of course, we knew it wouldn't be the wrong choice for her. We knew this was right. I didn't even consider moving her into our home or Shirley's home. My home had steps just to get into the house, which pretty much kept Mom from seeing the inside of our home. We had stairs going upstairs where the bedrooms were. My office was downstairs in the basement area, so there was another set of stairs. The washer and dryer were also down in the basement, so the washing of clothes all took place downstairs.

Mom was pretty independent. She did her own medications. No one helped her with that. I bought her a pill organizer, which I thought would help her even more. She loved it! I have no idea why she never had one of these in the past.

One of the big perks for Mom moving was the walk-in shower! She could take her own shower without any help from anyone else. That seems like such a small thing. After all, she had two ladies who came to help her with things like showers, cleaning, etc. But this was huge for her – that alone was worth the move.

I actually think she had gone a couple of weeks without a shower. It was so difficult for her to get into the tub-shower combination. She did sponge baths, but I don't think she took many showers.

Mom began putting on the breaks, however, at some point. Perhaps, it was overwhelming. I had to emphasize that I had reserved a room and it might not be available later. This was true. This particular facility stays rented at capacity. It is a good facility!

One recommendation by professionals who work in elder affairs is to emphasize how you feel rather than what you want for them. Elders often hide things from their children to protect them; and seniors may not be willing to even consider a change of residence.

Not all cases require a move. It is possible to bring in required services. For us, our issue was being so far away from our mom that we really had no idea what was really happening. You may live close enough to your elder to keep tabs on how they are doing. In this case, you may be able to manage your elder in their own home. Home health services can be provided by most visiting nurses associations (VNA). For more information, see *What Services Are Available?*

Getting your senior settled into their new surroundings is not merely the packing and moving of their things. However, packing and moving is a huge task: one that should involve your senior, as much as possible. While you know there are limits to what can fit into their new living arrangements, your elder may not be willing to part with some things. The best advice is to move it. These things can be downsized after the move.

When Shirley and I began packing up Mom, our intent was to help her take only what she truly wanted to keep. What we ended up doing was packing everything she wanted to keep. Shirley packed a couple of boxes of stuff that she wanted to keep. I packed things that I wanted to keep, as well. I just didn't have to mail them; I put them in with Mom's stuff, including a desk our grandfather had made.

There were more things than would fit into Mom's apartment. Mom realized that very quickly. Although she still wanted her dining room table, it just wouldn't fit. I still have it in my kitchen. I just couldn't part with it. It doesn't really fit into my kitchen, because I now have two tables. Mom's table has drop leaves so it can just be long and narrow, which is the only reason it is still where it is. I did give mom a smaller table; it was a portable table, which folds up. It fit into her apartment just right.

It is a good idea to create a familiar environment for your elder. You can do this easily, of course, by moving their familiar items. For example, Mom thought about moving one of her twin beds with her, instead of her own bed. While her bed was a full bed, I encouraged her to move it, because that was the mattress for which she was used to sleeping. It was a good call. She wouldn't have been as comfortable in the other bed.

She moved her sewing machine, but she didn't keep it. She realized that she wasn't going to be sewing. But it was her decision to let it go. It was also her decision to get rid of all her cookware, food, etc. Shirley and I did that only a few weeks ago when she visited. Most of the pots and pans and other kitchen accoutrements, we sent to Brian, Shirley's son who was just setting up housekeeping.

A lot of the food items were passed their expiration date, which has been a concern of mine from the start. However, Mom never cooked in her apartment. There wasn't any reason, because the facility provided all three meals.

If she didn't feel well enough to go downstairs, a meal was brought up to her. Mom thought she would cook, because she didn't have any idea that eating meals with other people would be so appealing. I knew that once Mom discovered a few friends, she'd be interested in continuing that friendship. I sat with the women during lunch quite often. I didn't eat very often, because I tend to get up later and have breakfast later. Mom enjoyed having me interact with her friends. She was proud to show off pictures of family, as well.

The settling in process is just that, a process. While getting her moved in was stage one, you have to be prepared for changes. Mom turned 92 in February, 2011. Changes in her health were probably more likely than if she were in her 70s or 80s. Keeping up with your elder's health is your job as the caregiver. You can't just move your elder into any facility and consider that you're done. You have to be their advocate, when they need that. You need to be aware of your elder's health. The facility will want a person to contact, of course, which probably means you! Sometimes their health can deteriorate overnight, so you need to stay in contact with your senior as much as possible.

While I do see being the caregiver as my job, it isn't an unpleasant one. Of course, my mom isn't ever cranky. She's just sweet. When she doesn't feel good, she usually apologizes. I realize that taking care of Mom was probably more pleasure than it would have been with Dad or maybe just about anyone. Dad was rarely ever sick. In fact, I can't remember my dad ever missing work because he was sick. However, when he didn't feel good, he was pretty cranky. Mom didn't pay a lot of attention to that, I suppose.

Elder care professionals encourage families to think of caring for an elder as part of a team. Care giving can be a burden, if only one sibling has taken it on. There are all different kinds of families, but each of your siblings loves your mom, dad, aunt, uncle or other elder, as well. Sometimes people choose to move the elder into their own home. This is quite a responsibility and it might also come with some needs for renovating parts of your home.

For example, a ramp might be needed to accommodate a walker or wheel chair. The bathroom may need some bars to make it safe. Your tub may need to be changed to a walk-in shower. The door to the bathroom and bedroom may need to be widened to accommodate a walker or wheel chair.

Who pays for the renovations? This is a decision that you and your siblings need to decide. There could be a lot of resentment, if you have to bear the entire financial burden. On the flip side, perhaps your siblings don't agree that you should be reimbursed. Iron these issues out prior to moving your elder, if possible.

Another option is to check for services through your senior center. Sometimes there are volunteers who will modify your bathroom by putting up the bars in the bathroom. I don't think anyone will change out the bathtub to a walk-in shower for free, but it doesn't hurt to check it out. Medicare will pay for a lot of things to help the livability level of your elder. Other non-profits in your area may also offer some assistance, especially when there are extenuating circumstances.

If your senior is moving in with you and you are providing some of the care giving, you might discuss payment for these services with your senior and your siblings. Again, to avoid family rifts, make sure all your siblings are on the same page.

Guilt can also come along with decisions to move your elder. For example, if you promised never to put your mom into a nursing home, and now you find that the level of care warrants the nursing home bypassing assisted living or other levels of care. You might feel guilty about doing exactly what you had promised not to do.

Here's the deal! We were lucky with our mom. Assisted living is not appropriate for all elders. If your elder is fairly healthy and independent, the assisted living may work for them. However, if your elder really needs skilled nursing care, the assisted living will not work for them. Assisted living only assists with certain things. There isn't an aide for each resident around the clock. There are aides that are there all day and all night, but the deep night shift (typically, 11 p.m. to 7 a.m.) is usually staffed for minimum needs.

You can contract for other services, but if you need someone more or less 24/7, the nursing home may be your best choice. Even nursing homes cannot always provide the level of care you feel your senior needs. Explore all the options prior to signing contracts and leases.

Assisted living is also expensive and not every senior can afford this level of care, which sometimes forces family members to take their elder into their household. If you feel this is the decision you need to make, check out VNA (visiting nurses association) services in your area. You may qualify for housekeeping, personal care, and nursing services for your senior. Sometimes these services are free or are covered under Medicare.

What is critical is that you and your siblings get on the same page about the care for your senior. Mom or Dad or other elder may not be mentally capable of making a decision. If your elder suffers from any form of dementia, he or she may need specialized care.

Dementia, such as Alzheimer's, often causes seniors to need a locked-in facility. Some assisted living facilities offer this sort of arrangement. However, some seniors may have other issues, as well, and may need nursing home care.

Caring for a parent or other elder in your home is a lot of work. If dementia is one of your senior's issues, this can be difficult. While we start out thinking we can handle almost anything, if your senior cannot even remember your name, this can become a huge barrier in caring for your loved one. At first, you don't think about it, but dementia can make an elder very demanding. Be willing to revisit their care and their living arrangements.

If your parent or elder has little to no money, it does seem like a logical course to take on their care single handed. However, sometimes that is not what your senior needs at all! Keeping your elder feeling as independent as possible should be one of your goals. How will you handle your life, when you have to bathe and clothe your senior, as well as, make sure they take their medications accurately, do their laundry, make their meals, and possibly even change their briefs for them (due to incontinence). It's like having a baby to care for, but instead of easily being able to pick up and care for a baby, you need to do similar things with a full-size adult.

Moving your elder takes a lot of thought and pre-arranging. You don't want to have to make two moves, so check with doctors about your senior's abilities and medical needs. Before moving Mom up to Massachusetts, I talked to Mom's doctor about traveling and moving. He thought it was a great idea!

Back: Odell Neel Jones, Emily Jane Neel Sherrill
Front: Mary Frances Gross, Olivia Marchbanks Neel

# HOW TO FIND APPROPRIATE HOUSING

Finding appropriate housing can be confusing. Not all facilities bill their services in the same manner, which can make comparisons like apples and motorcycles. Where to start is often the hard part, but you don't have to do it alone. There are some non-profit groups that can help. Here is a list of some:

A Place for Mom - www.aplaceformom.com
Housing Options Made Easy - www.housing-options.com
My Senior Care - www.myseniorcare.com
Seniors for Living - www.seniorsforliving.com
Senior Outlook - www.senioroutlook.com
Senior Resources - www.seniorresource.com

I used *A Place for Mom*, but ended up searching to see what was around me, as well. I actually picked a place that wasn't on their list. I will say, however, that it was helpful to hear what they had to say. It helped jump start me into the process.

It comes down to what services are important to you and your elder. What does your elder need help with now and how likely will these needs change? I can answer that one for you. They will change! They will need more services, which you need to know how the facility works that. If your elder is independent when entering a facility, they may stay that way for quite some time. However, illness happens. Elders don't necessarily bounce back, and as they get older their health does decline. But each person weathers this in his or her own way. There's no cookie cutter answer for how your elder will be at any stage. I began this book by saying that from the moment we are born, we are growing toward the day we die. We don't have any control over when that happens. Your elder needs encouragement to live their life to the fullest. For most, living in a senior community with lots of activities helps them to enjoy their life more. However, the enjoyment of anything is up to the individual, their likes and dislikes, and their personalities.

Mom loved living in the assisted living community. She loved eating meals with her friends. She shared pictures of her family with these friends. She loved all the staff and they loved her back. Of course, Mom was a social person.

She loved dressing up and looking nice. I'm not sure, if she even understood how starved she was for having a social life with people her own age. She had been fairly isolated living in rural Tennessee. While when they first moved there, they had friends for whom they socialized. As they all got older, their friends moved closer to their children or died off.

At the assisted living facility, loads of activities were available, but Mom did not necessarily go to them. She might have when she was just a little younger and little less medically challenged. She liked Church Service and there were several parties that she attended. But she needed her naps.

At 92, Mom wasn't going to get in better condition. She had congestive heart failure for which the only cure would have been surgery. Since Mom was already on oxygen and had been for about three years, surgery wasn't really a possible solution.

As Mom's congestive heart failure became more serious, she wasn't able to do some of the things she had in the past. Putting her shoes on caused her to be out of breath. At an assisted living facility, this is not unusual. There are aides that help the residents with things like this.

Some facilities bill charges for the aides based on actual time, but that's hard to keep track of. For example, coming in to help a resident with their shoes only takes a couple of minutes. If you're billed for a minimum of a quarter of an hour for any portion of 15 or less minutes, then having to have your shoes put on can cost an awfully lot of money. Facilities that include within their fee up to a certain number of hours, such as 7 hours per week or an hour per day, make more sense.

As service needs change, you may need to understand how to renegotiate the fees, if necessary. The most common way to change the services is to contract outside the facility with the VNA (Visiting Nurses Association) or Hospice or other independent aide services.

A good facility will help you find the resources you need. In fact, the nursing staff (nurses and aides) may know before you know that your elder needs additional services.

Assisted living facilities are not nursing homes. You cannot expect round-the-clock care. While there are aides available around the clock, it doesn't equate to round-the-clock care for any individual. For example, there may be more than 100 residents, so no one aide can spend their entire shift with one resident.

This is an important issue to understand. If your elder needs someone with them at all times, you'll probably need to contract for that service outside the facility or move them into a nursing home, depending on finances and individual needs. At $19 an hour, an unskilled aide can be with your senior for any number of hours. The toll racks up quickly, so you don't want to be frivolous, but you do want to stay safe.

We were fortunate; I got Hospice in place quickly when it was evident that Mom needed more services. While the catalyst for getting Hospice was Mom's plea of not going to the hospital again, it proved to be one of the best things that I did. We might have been able to do some similar types of services going another way, but Hospice was a good fit.

There was a Hospice Aide that came to bathe or assist in the shower two times a week. We did contract for an aide, in addition to the facility's aides and Hospice, because I wanted someone to be in the room with Mom. I didn't want her to be alone. But I only organized this for a very short time. Had Mom needed this sort of care for months on end, we would have run out of money or we would have had to put her in a nursing home. I'm glad I didn't have to move her again.

In all honesty, if she would have needed that level of care long-term, I probably would have had to make a different decision. However, she did not. It all depends on finances available and the services needed. You have to make smart decisions based on what you know about your elder's level of needs and be flexible enough to change as your elder's needs change.

When I originally chose Forge Hill Senior Living, I chose it because it was close by. I was moving Mom up from Tennessee. It didn't make sense to put her in a facility that was several towns away. This one was in my town and only about five minutes away from my home. That made the most sense. Trust yourself to make decisions like that. Financially, I found them to all be in the same or nearly the same ball-park range. They were dissimilar in services offered a la carte. However, most of the assisted living facilities also allow for outside services to be brought in. We had a VNA (Visiting Nurses Association) that came in to work with Mom right away. When we went on Hospice that VNA was replaced by a Hospice nurse/nurse practitioner.

My experience was fairly typical in locating a facility. I got leads from *A Place for Mom*, called them, made an appointment to visit, and visited the facility. One of the facilities sent me home with a whole fresh baked apple pie from their dining room. Impressive! And I nearly chose them because of that, but when it got down to the bare facts and needs, I chose using this checklist:

- How quickly could I get to Mom?
- How comfortable does the room/apartment feel?
- Price range vs services – are they doable?
- How friendly was the facility?
- How friendly did the staff seem?
- What options are available, if Mom runs low on money?
- If she gets very sick, does she have to go to nursing home?
- What does the nursing care consist of?
- How are meals handled?
- How are activities handled?
- What other services, such as beauty shop, are available?

Finding a suitable housing situation should not be taken lightly. Assisted living facilities aren't cheap housing choices. Senior housing can mean small independent apartments with a subsidy that allows people who only have a social security benefit to live fairly inexpensively. However, these facilities do not offer any assistance.

When you have helped your elder get into a senior housing situation, you will need to be very involved in what's happening in their life. Elders can change needs quickly. Even if your elder is in a senior apartment style living situation, because they cannot afford assisted living, you can still contract for other services. Because their income will be low, some services may be free or nearly free. Health aides may be contracted with to help your elder with showers or bathing and for cleaning. You may need to do your elder's shopping and take them to doctor's appointments. However, in some places there are services that can be contracted for these services, as well. Again, it depends on how much money you have; what services are available in your area; and what services your senior needs.

Choosing housing must incorporate your elder's health and abilities along with their financial wherewithal. Having all the legal documents in place will also aid you in finding the right options. Legal documents usually include power of attorney, health care proxy and will. Talking with an estate attorney should ensure that you get all the documents needed for the state in which your elder lives or will be living. In some cases, you may be able to get a nurse or social worker to help with assessments and placement.

The basic choices of housing include:

**Alzheimer's/Dementia Residences** – these facilities offer a home-like atmosphere, specialize in Dementia and Alzheimer's, and provide more one-on-one care than Assisted Living Facilities. These facilities are licensed by the state and may not be available everywhere.

**Assisted Living** – this is a residential facility with efficiency, one-bedroom, or two bedroom apartments. Residents can live independent, meaning no help from aides, to needing assistance (requiring a certain number of hours per week).

**Continuing Care Retirement Community** – this is a community that offers life care, which means that there are multiple levels of care beginning with a private residence through nursing home care.

**Hospice House** – in some places, Hospice operates houses where patients come to live at the end of their life.

**Nursing Home** – this is a skilled nursing center, where patients may receive such skilled services as wound care, cardiac care, pulmonary care, and stroke care.

**Private Home** – this can be a place where your elder has lived all her life. Keeping your senior in that home will require contracting for outside help.

**Residential or Foster Care** – this is similar to the Alzheimer's and Dementia Residences; they offer a home-like atmosphere and more one-on-one care.

The type of care your senior needs determines what sort of facility for which you are looking. At the beginning of this chapter, I listed some non-profit agencies which can assist you in your search.

# WHAT SERVICES ARE AVAILABLE?

Varying services are available in towns and cities across America. Elder services are definitely not standard services you can count on no matter where your elder is living or where you need to move them. In many areas there are Councils on Aging (COA), which can give you a list of all the services in your area.

If you don't have a COA near you, finding all the services you need, may be a bit more difficult. However, check with churches and other resource centers. My Senior Care Guide (www.myseniorcareguide.com) can help you find services all over the country.

Maybe you aren't sure what services are even possible? Let's take a look at some of the services that you might need or have available. Again, services can vary from town-to-town and state-to-state.

In-home services can include a professional companion, whose job would be to make sure safety standards would be upheld. This person might also perform some light housekeeping, dressing, bathing, laundry, meal preparation, and shopping. Shopping services may carry a mileage charge due to the companion using his/her own transportation. Sometimes the shopping services can include taking the elder shopping, which is great if your elder is capable of shopping.

Before securing a professional companion for your elder, make sure you understand what services you are contracting with the companion. Also, note that a professional companion is not trained in performing any medical procedures and should not be responsible for medications. If the companion services are combined with a VNA (visiting nursing association) service, medications would fall into the VNA responsibilities. This can consist of filling the elder's med box weekly. The companion then might only need to remind the elder to take them at the appointed time.

A **companion** can help families with respite care or long-term care. Live-in companions should be given time off, which means you should be hiring a second companion to cover that time, if you are not available to fill in this time.

**In-home health care** is one of the staples of senior care. Professional medical care at your elder's home, which also includes any senior housing, including an assisted living facility, is the key to home health care. Your senior's physician normally prescribes or recommends in-home medical care prior to your securing the services.

However, if you feel the care is needed, you can check with your elder's physician, provided you are the health care proxy or have been given permission by your elder. Most physicians take privacy seriously.

Remember that doctors don't always see their patients regularly enough to make this decision for every patient. Some elders decline considerably before anyone becomes aware that more care needs to be arranged.

If you are a family member of an elder, make sure that someone in your family is following closely with your aging senior. Care changes can often happen quickly, which leaves your elder at risk for hurting themselves, missing medications or taking them too frequently, and a host of other negative possibilities. Take care of the elders in your family by staying tuned in to their lives.

**Skilled nursing care** includes medications, wound care, recovery from surgery or illnesses. These services are often covered through a VNA. However, hospice also offers similar nursing care. Specialized medical care including physical therapy, occupational therapy, and speech therapy, brings in different levels of skilled care to help when needed, as well.

**Hospice** can come into the home (any senior housing or assisted living facility) when a senior has an illness from which they cannot recover within the next six months. This is a very broad definition. Often hospice stays longer, more than a year, in some cases. Sometimes hospice comes and goes when the patient gets better. Check with hospice or your elder's physician, if you feel your senior needs this service.

**Certified Nursing Aides or Assistants (CNAs)** usually hold a certification, which are often issued by the American Red Cross after completion of training. CNAs are regulated state by state. They often help with personal care in hospitals, nursing homes and assisted living facilities.

**Home Health Aides and Personal Care Aides** help people who are disabled, chronically ill, or cognitively impaired and older adults, who need assistance to live in their own homes, senior housing, or assisted living facilities. These are the people who also assist people in hospices and day programs. They help people with disabilities go to work and remain engaged in their communities, as well as the physically and mentally disabled. However, for this book, we are focused on the elderly, who could also be physically or mentally disabled.

**Aides** provide light housekeeping and homemaking tasks such as laundry, change bed linens, shop for food, plan and prepare meals. They may also assist with personal bathing and grooming or even accompany their elder to doctor's appointments and other errands. In general, home health aides and personal or home care aides have similar job duties. Home health aides typically work for certified home health or hospice agencies that receive government funding; and therefore, must comply with government regulations to receive funding. This means that they must work under the direct supervision of a medical professional, usually a nurse. These aides keep records of services performed and of clients' condition and progress.

**Licensed Nursing Staff** includes **Registered Nurses, Licensed Vocational Nurses** or **Licensed Practical Nurses**. These trained nurses are generally the case managers for their patients and arrange for health aides and other care, as needed. The nursing staff stays in touch with the doctor and follows their orders. They take blood and drop it off at a lab and order refills, as needed or prescribed by the physician. They work with the families to provide the best care possible.

Deciding what care your elder needs does not rest solely on your shoulders. However, you may know best, so don't second guess yourself. If you love your elder and your elder loves you, you will arrange for all the legal papers, understand the wishes of your elder, and be the best advocate for your elder. Accompanying your elder to doctor's appointments help you understand their needs, plus it gives your elder another ear for listening to what it is the doctor wishes for them to do.

My experience with Mom was both rewarding and eye-opening. You see, on one hand, Mom had all her faculties about her. She was as smart a woman as she always was. She had lost none of her mind, which was a beautiful thing. However, she had some communication issues. Sometimes her hearing aids just didn't seem to be working well.

I suppose after I moved my mom up to Massachusetts, I pretty well devoted my life to her. I saw her almost every day, and if I didn't see her, I most surely talked to her on the phone. I probably knew Mom better than anyone. She had good days and bad days, but who doesn't? I loved my mom with all my heart and what I wanted most for her was to live her life to the fullest extent that she could. When she wasn't feeling well, I took her to the doctor or did whatever needed to be done to make her feel better.

Sometimes when I took her to the doctor, she didn't always answer the doctor correctly. It wasn't that she was trying to hide something; she simply didn't understand what was asked. So I acted as translator for her a lot of times. When she had to go the emergency room, the same thing would happen. Especially, when she didn't have her hearing aids, she would answer wrong – obviously wrong, which I knew meant that she didn't understand the question. I also would prompt her sometimes to get her to tell the doctors or nurses what was going on. I tried not to jump in and have the conversation with them by cutting her out of the conversation. At times, that is what will happen.

Actually medical people understand working with elders and will speak louder and get closer to them to talk. I have to say that the medical staff at the hospital was very thorough about educating Mom about her medical issues. They printed out all sorts of information for Mom to read; and she willingly read all of it.

Mom had congestive heart failure, a condition that worsened. In Tennessee, she had one leaky valve. Once she started having to go to the hospital in 2011, she had three leaky valves. Two leaked considerably; one leaked moderately. So three out of the four heart valves were leaking, which meant that her heart had to work extra hard to pump blood, and much of it leaked back into the heart instead flowing through the veins and arteries.

My mom's heart simply wore out. It had to beat so hard that it simply couldn't keep up. On the day Mom passed, her breathing was very slow, but her heart was beating very fast.

Understanding what her condition was, helped me understand the level of care and services that she required. While her situation obviously changed due to more leaking of her heart valves, her care also needed to change to keep up with it.

**Adult Day Care** or **Senior Day Care** programs offer care during the day. Often the participants in this care have family members that provide the primary care in their own home. However, these family members probably have full time jobs, which mean the elder must be able to stay at home alone. Adult Day Care is warranted when the senior is a safety risk when left alone, unable to structure their own daily activities, and suffers from isolation.

**Adult Day Care** programs are licensed state by state and are not available everywhere. In lieu of a day program, companion service or a health aide can be contracted through a VNA or similar service.

**Senior in-home care** refers to caregivers coming to the senior's home to take care of a range of needs. From companionship to personal care to medical care, senior in-home care covers a wide range of tasks that are specifically geared toward helping seniors in the comfort of their own homes. These services are also available to seniors in assisted living facilities. Popular in-home services include the following:

**Senior In-Home Care** - in-home care for seniors: companionship, personal care, transportation services, etc.

**Senior In-Home Health Care – Medical** - in-home medical care for seniors: skilled nursing care, physical therapy, occupational therapy, speech therapy etc.

**Senior Home Repair & Maintenance** - home maintenance and remodeling for seniors: disability remodel, handyman help, maid service, etc.

**Senior Care** - care for seniors: companionship, personal care, transportation services, medical services, etc.

**Geriatric Care Consultant** - consultation care services for seniors who would like to learn more about care options available to them.

**Personal Emergency Response System** - allows individuals to call for help in case of emergency by use of a necklace or wristband.

**Senior Housing** - provides safe and comfortable housing for seniors who either need extra help in their day-to-day lives, require the 24-hour skilled nursing care or are looking for an active retirement community.

**Disability Planner** - specialist in disability planning help you plan out changes in your current living facility, such as your house. This might include a ramp, widening doorways, bars in the bathroom and shower. The Disability Planner does not actually build it, but will help design a plan for improving your home so you can stay in it.

**Maid Service** - routine cleaning of the home's interior areas.

# WHEN LIFE LEAVES, THEN WHAT?

Mom's Hospice Health Aide came in today. A couple of the other aides had already come in and washed her up, put her in a Johnny, and put nice-smelling lotion on her. I pulled out her prayer shawl. We covered her with her sheets and blanket and I spread out the shawl over her. The Health Aide painted her fingernails. It was such a sweet gesture.

I told her how beautiful she was, rubbed her cheeks, kissed her softly, moistened her mouth, and put moistener on her lips. Then, I held her hand and told her that I loved her. I reminded her that it was her $69^{th}$ wedding anniversary and that if Dad was there for her, she could choose to go with him.

Mainly, I watched her breathe. I listened to her breathe. And I knew the room was full of Angels. I could feel them.

The woman who has done Mom's hair for the last 10 months came in to visit. We couldn't get Mom to open her eyes. We were just chatting, when I heard her take a deep breath and let it out. I turned and watched her chest; it wasn't going up and down. The room seemed so empty. I checked her out. No breath. No heartbeat. She was gone just like that. The hairdresser was concerned that she had kept me from that moment. I assured her that she had not. I don't think I knew how in tune I had been with her.

I called the front desk to inform them of mother's passing. It was no time before the aides came in. I called Hospice. The aides stayed with me. I called Joyce. Later, after Barbara, our Hospice nurse, came in and filled out all the right papers, I called the funeral home.

Miss Odell had chosen her own time to go. Did she go off into eternity with the love of her life? That's the way I would like to remember it. Is there any evidence that this is what happened? Well, of course, not! There is no way that I could claim such a thing without any doubts. But let's step back a moment.

Miss Odell fell in love with Harold Jones about 72 years ago. She first met Harold at work in a bakery. She was the icing/frosting girl (I use both terms: icing is what one would say in the South; frosting is the preferred word in the North). He was the grease-the-pan man. They were a beautiful couple!

Wedding Picture
Odell Neel and Harold Jones
Married on Aug. 9, 1942

"I kept noticing him and liked him," she'd say. "He would whistle and I loved the sound of it, as he was really good! One day, he asked me for a date, which I accepted. We went to a show *The Great Waltz* with Mario Lanza singing in it."

After the show, they went to Triple X Root Beer for some frosty coated glasses of Root Beer to drink. He hadn't been in Waco long and was living with his grandparents. He had used their car to take Miss Odell on the date. Unfortunately, while they were in seeing the movie, someone stole the spare tire. So much for another date in that car! Not only did he not have use of a car, he would have to replace the spare.

Wages in those days were very poor. Mom explains that she only made $10 for the week. I don't know how long Dad had to work to pay for the spare. However, it did not keep Miss Odell and Harold apart.

They had to double date with a neighbor of Harold's named Lloyd and his girlfriend, but it wasn't long before Harold bought a Model T Coupe. Mom says, "Then we dated every weekend. We all got paid on Friday, so we'd usually be together then and on Saturday night. Sometimes on Sunday afternoons we were together, but bakery days started on Sunday for Monday's business, so I often had to work myself."

For years, Harold and Miss Odell would double date. They doubled with one of Miss Odell's sisters, Evelyn. There were four sisters. Miss Odell was the oldest. The sisters were: Evelyn, Emily, and the baby, Mary Frances. They didn't have to spend loads of money on dates, in fact, they often doubled with Evelyn and James to go on picnics, swimming, and just hanging out having fun. About a year later, Evelyn and James married and moved away to San Antonio, Texas.

"Harold and I went places—just the two of us," Miss Odell explains. "Harold and I had been in love a couple of years by then. I did not go with anyone else but him from the time we started dating. We had gone together three-and-a-half years by the time we got married on August 9, 1942.

Harold had to go into the service—the army. He was in limited service because his left eyesight was really bad, so he was with hospital units."

Sixty-nine years ago to the date of her death, they were married. How romantic is that!

Harold and Odell
shortly after Harold's retirement

## Everlasting Sweethearts

In Frankie's Bakery, the two did meet:
She, the icing girl, confection sweet;
He, the grease-the-pan baking sort of man,
Who baked their eternal love plan.

The man wooed his gal with a whistling tune.
Did he know it would cause her to swoon?
No one rushed the affectionate courtship.
Did the war bring thoughts of a warship?

Miss Odell doted upon Harold's charm.
With her sweet beauty, she did disarm.
Their deep love would last for eternity.
It was August 9, 1942.

They began their married life together.
Despite war and rations, their fervor
Held tight to their lives through separation.
With child, a family they had begun.

He, near Chicago; and she in Texas –
Long distance lovers are so fearless.
Miss Odell had not lived with snow before,
Undaunted, she moved: even the score.

The army shipped Harold to Paris, France.
In letters he'd write, she found romance.
He returned after the war was over.
A family, they made with honor.

The man wooed his gal with a whistling tune.
Did he know it would cause her to swoon?
Three years now, he left this worldly life.
At 92, she said, he'd come for his wife.

And on August 9, 2011,
Sixty-nine years to the blessed day,
She took one last earthly breath and left us
To live in eternal love with him.

The man wooed his gal with a whistling tune.
Did he know it would cause her to swoon?
Miss Odell doted upon Harold's charm.
With her sweet beauty, she did disarm.

Now and forever, they walk the heavens;
Holding hands as loving light beacons.
Their earthly life a memory in our hearts:
Everlasting romantic sweethearts.

Miss Odell with granddaughter Erin (2006)

Miss Odell in her Tennessee home (2006)

Miss Odell in her Tennessee home (2008)

Miss Odell in her Massachusetts apartment (2010)

# THE MOURNING

When someone dies, people mourn. It is healthy to mourn. You cannot escape it. You might prolong it or delay it, but grieving is a process that you cannot avoid.

There are five stages of grief:
1. **Denial:** "This can't be happening to me."
2. **Anger:** "WHY is this happening? Who is to blame?"
3. **Bargaining:** "Make this not happen, and in return I will ____."
4. **Depression:** "I'm too sad to do anything."
5. **Acceptance:** "I'm at peace with what happened."

There is no way to predict exactly how long this process is going to take you. You cannot rush it or put it off. You can ignore it, but it will still happen. It may happen when you least suspect it.

Mom's passing was not a surprise. I knew it was just a matter of time. Mom knew it was a matter of time. Did it help me jump start the grief process? No. It made me strong enough to be there for Mom through the end. It made me strong enough to make all the arrangements for Mom and pack up her things. It made me strong enough to handle my grief, whenever and however the grief comes.

For the last couple of weeks of Mom's life, I spent every day, all day, with her. When she was awake, I would talk to her, kiss her, and do Reiki on her. I loved my mom deeply. To pack up all her things required my being strong. It also was therapy and comforting to be in her space, although I knew she was not there any more.

The week after Mom died was supposed to have been a vacation week for Joyce and me. We were supposed to go to Ferry Beach, a Unitarian Universalist camp and conference center for Women's Week. I wasn't ready to go to camp when we were originally supposed to go, so we didn't go. When all was packed in Mom's apartment, I was more ready. I tried to get it moved, but we were battling rain. I was able to let that part go, and travel to see our friends, most of whom we only see this one week a year.

We went to Ferry Beach on Tuesday night. We got to camp in time to catch the last hour of playing Women's Jeopardy, a women's week tradition. I still wasn't sure how I really felt about anything. It was the right thing to go to camp.

It was a laid back few days - Wednesday through Friday. One of the activities that I attended was a healing circle. I was able to cry and reached deep into sorrow. I needed to feel that. I had been so strong that I had not allowed myself to feel the loss. It was only a slight dip into the abyss of grief that I knew I would feel.

Had I experienced the denial? No, not really. I didn't feel denial. I didn't feel angry; and I didn't feel the bargaining or the depression. I felt the acceptance of Mom's death, yet I knew I had not yet begun my grief process.

Everyone handles grief and mourns in a different way. While the stages of grief are just some of the emotions you might feel, you may not follow that route. And...it's okay!

According to hospice.net, adjusting to life without your loved one can be painful. While there are general guidelines for how grief affects us, our emotions cannot be predicted. Each of us must follow our own journey through grief. There are no complete lists of experiences that comprise grief.

Because the death of someone causes a separation, it is often necessary to find a new direction for your emotional energy. It doesn't mean you have to forget your lost loved one. It just means that mourning means you need to find emotional satisfaction through interaction with others. In other words, all that emotional energy that you devoted to the person who died, you need to give to other people and activities.

According to SeasonsHospice.org, when we lose a loved one, we find ways to accept the reality and gradually discover the extent of our losses. This process, however, takes time and energy.

Since we are still among the living, our journey continues. It is essential that we continue our life with all of what life holds. Our loved ones do not ask us to take the journey with them to the afterlife but to be there with them through their end of life. They want us to live our lives to the fullest. They do not want us to stop living.

Because we often love deeply, we tend to get caught in our grief. While the grief process is unpredictable, we cannot speed it up or slow it down. The process is something we must allow to be present in our life. Yes, that may mean that we feel sad or angry or even depressed. I'm not suggesting that we relish in our feelings unnecessarily, but what we feel, we feel. We need to indulge ourselves to just be how we are.

The reverse is also true. We can avoid the pain by avoiding the grief. But we cannot heal and get on with our life unless we face our grief and allow the process of grieving.

According to griefandhealing.org, one myth is the need for being strong. Feeling sad, frightened or lonely is a normal reaction to loss. Showing your emotions is not a sign of weakness. While you don't need to "protect" your family or friends by putting on a brave front, crying doesn't mean you are weak. You don't need to "protect" your family or friends by putting on a brave front. Showing your true feelings can help you and others.

When we are sad, crying is a normal response. It's not the only feeling. Those who don't cry may feel the pain just as deeply as others. However, they may simply express it in different ways. There is no right or wrong time frame for grieving. It takes a different amount of time for different folks. It is also good to talk about your loss.

When you choose to move on with your life, it simply means that you've accepted your loved one's death. It is not a sign that you are forgetting your loved one. You keep the memories alive. You tell the stories of your loved one to generations that come after you. In doing this, your loved one is very much alive in the hearts and minds of those you touch.

As a Unitarian Universalist, I know people whose spiritual philosophy is widely diverse. Some people don't believe there is an afterlife. Some may believe there is something, but they may not have a name for it. Heaven is a Christian invention, and as such, it is limiting. Only those who have accepted Jesus Christ as their savior can enter Heaven. That leaves out quite a few people! Jews, for example, don't recognize Jesus as the Messiah; therefore, they could not accept Jesus as the Christ or Heaven. Yet, Heaven is talked about in the old Testament. Buddhists might find Jesus' teachings to be enlightened, but they cannot accept Jesus as their savior, which means they couldn't enter Heaven. Buddhists would be fine with that, since they work toward enlightenment and not a cushy palace in Heaven. Just as people's ideas about the afterlife differ, their ideas about death and dying differ.

Your spiritual choices may not match others, nor should they. We are each an individual and should be respected as such. If I'm a square peg, I probably am not going to fit into the nice round hole you've dug for me.

We do not have to agree spiritually to support each other through the grieving process. We do need to be respectful that each person is different and is in a different place along their spiritual path. Where you are on your spiritual path may reflect where you are in the grieving process.

If you are struggling with the idea of an afterlife, it might be harder for you to come to terms with your loved one's death. For example, I do not see myself as Christian, because I feel that limits my beliefs. I consider myself to be a pantheist, which means that I believe in a world view that includes more than one Deity. I also think that these Deities are all part of the mystery that some people call God. As a Religious Educator, I've had the opportunity to explore most World Religions to some degree or the other.

The more I learned, the more I found these religions to be similar. They used different terminology, and they interpret things differently. But they all have a golden rule that is similar to: do unto others as you would have them do unto you.

My point is that we all are different, individual people with a variety of spiritual views, which means we all interpret the end of life from a distinctive and unique place. I do not judge where people are spiritually, but encourage people to be gentle on themselves and others. Making sense of your loved one's death can be an impossible task. Facing the finality of our own lives can be frightening.

Talking about your loved one with others can help ease the pain. It's okay not to have a definite vision of the afterlife or believe that it exists. However, the folks who do believe in a life after death are more often able to mourn and get on with their lives quicker.

According to *The Forum*, published by the Association for Death Education and Counseling, "while expressed differently, each person's spirituality is a way of reconnecting the individual with the transcendent; "to know the life that transcends death." Therefore, it is necessary to incorporate spirituality into end of life programs. Not only is it necessary for spiritual concerns to be present for the individual but for the entire families of those who are dying so that they might experience a good death. For those who are non-religious, spiritual resources may include: finding purpose and meaning; forgiving and receiving forgiveness; maintaining hope; saying goodbye; and coming to terms with whatever it is they believe happens after death.

Let's back track a bit and look at the roles that religions plays with regard to death. Recently spirituality is on the upswing and is often used interchangeably with religion. However, the two terms are more opposites than synonyms. Religious traditions often overshadow those who are professionally involved with death and bereavement, according to *The Forum*. "Sometimes this takes the form of a strong religious outlook among those who perceive their care of the dying as a vocation or calling. Sometimes it is more ambiguous. Signs of this hidden legacy appear when presenters at meetings say of themselves, `I'm what used to be called a 'lapsed Catholic,' or `I'm a recovering Baptist.'

"Religion can also be present when theories borrow and adapt frameworks that originated in religious contexts, but that have now taken on a life within psychology, or other seemingly secular disciplines," states *The Forum*. "When we think of spirituality as universal, beyond or outside of culture and history, we make such legacies invisible. Spirituality may play a key role in the end of life and the following grief. "Indeed, for many individuals, spirituality may play the most important role in end-of-life care via the meaning it provides and in the hope it offers beyond the medical cure: the hope for an afterlife, hope for salvation, and hope for nirvana."

We should also explore the contemporary idea of *coming to terms with loss* or *dying as the final stage of growth*. This language was first forged in the early 20th century, by liberal Protestantism, where a focus on *the dignity and worth of human personality* and *individual growth* became dominant themes of faith. But we also have to understand that death is not a science. While we all grieve differently, including the loved one who is dying, the most we can offer each other is support and a listening ear.

"I've come to believe that the need for spirituality — belief in a higher power — must be inherent in humans," says Edward T. Creagan, M.D. in his Stress Blog, published on the MayoClinic.com Website, "much like the need for water and oxygen. We may have different belief systems, but at the end of the day we all reach for something over and above ourselves."

Tibetan Buddhist teacher Sogyal Rinpoche wrote in *The Tibetan Book of Living and Dying:*

> *There would be no chance of getting to know death if it happened only once. But fortunately, life is nothing but a continuing dance of birth and death, a dance of change. Every time I hear the rush of a mountain stream, or the waves crashing on the shore, or my own heartbeat, I hear the sound of impermanence. These changes, these small deaths, are our living links with death. They are death's pulse, death's heartbeat, prompting us to let go of all the things we cling to.*

According to HarleyHahn.com, coming to terms with our own mortality can be frightening. One of his readers responded with the following quote:

> *Well, with the thought of no after-life, no soul, and no spiritual being engraved in my brain; it has brought down my good expectations of death by 100%, but it has made me appreciate life a whole lot more. So just live life to its fullest, enjoy it while you are here. Now I know and understand when people would say that life is the greatest gift of them all. - Joel*

According to Dharma-Haven.org, we should focus on life rather than death. The Website has written:

> *Truly respecting death and its inevitability brings, paradoxically, a relaxing of the fear of death, along with a heightened sense of the importance of life and of what we choose to do with the time we have. The fact that any particular person is going to die or has already died is no ones fault -- it is a necessary part of being alive.*

Most of these quotes can be easily pulled up on Google. They show that people have thought deeply about death and dying. Some wrote about dying on a personal level, others wrote about their experiences with the death of someone close. However, they all offer an insight into the process of *coming to terms with loss*. As I wrote earlier in this chapter, loss is part of living. We cannot live our entire lives without having to let go of something in order to grasp onto something else. We constantly deal with the issues of death, yet simultaneously, we try to avoid it.

Mourning the death of a loved one brings up many spiritual and religious issues for people. Having someone to whom you can discuss these issues, such as a bereavement counselor or minister, can be helpful as you go through the process. Hospice services often include bereavement services.

As you think about all the things you've let go of in your life, so that you can take on something new, perhaps that will be comforting to embrace the changes that your loss will mean in your life. Even when we clean out our closet so we can buy some new fashion, we are making changes.

Theresa Tyagi Kersten writes in the Journal for Vibrational/Flower Essences:

> *Beings are birth and death. Though most people will face both and not seek to plumb the depths of transformation and illumination that are available at those times, some may choose otherwise. Both experiences offer the opportunity to transcend our attachments to our view of ourselves as being our bodies and ego. Instead, they can provide gateway experiences to the realization of ourselves as souls who are deeply connected to the totality of creation.*

In the Buddhist world view, there is no death, only transition. Deepak Chopra tells us:

> *Human beings are made of body, mind and spirit.*
> *Of these, spirit is primary,*
> *for it connects us to the source of everything,*
> *the eternal field of consciousness."*
> *and that....*
> *"Each of us is here to discover our true Self...*
> *that essentially we are spiritual beings*
> *who have taken manifestation in physical form...*
> *that we're not human beings that have occasional spiritual experiences*
> *that we're spiritual beings that have occasional human experiences....*

As naturally spirit-filled beings, we have a plethora of religious and spiritual beliefs. The good news is that diversity is good, because that allows all of us to be authentically who we are. We live, we die, we celebrate, and we mourn. Life brings us many experiences. Many sages have said that life doesn't bring us anything we cannot handle. While some would argue with that, I would say that when we face difficult things and make it through, we grow. Growth in spirit and character can only make us better humans.

How we handle life's tough events says a lot about us. This doesn't mean that when we're sad or whatever, we shouldn't feel what we feel. What we need to do is live through it: survive. We become stronger when we do. Through our experiences, we can also help others. Mourning is part of life.

Death is part of life. It always has been. However, in our contemporary society, we tend to ignore losses. When we refuse to acknowledge either the gains or losses that are part of our life, we choose to accept only parts of our life. In generations of the past, we embraced the passing of the seasons – be it the weather or life cycles.

In our previous American farming culture, we often had several generations living together. Children grew up with parents and grandparents and sometimes great-grandparents. As the elders aged, the family took care of them. When they died, the family celebrated their life.

When we have the opportunity to mourn our loved ones, we remember our memories; therefore, celebrate who our loved ones were. Our relationship is commemorated, and we can rejoice in what we remember and hold forever in our heart. Because by recalling those memories and stories over and over, we keep them alive in our lives and the lives of those who hear the stories that you share.

Connie Dunn

# ABOUT AUTHOR

Connie Dunn is a Certified Master Life Coach, Certified Master Neuro Linguistic Programming Practitioner, Master Reiki Practitioner, Vibrational Therapy (includes Color Healing, Sound Therapy, Healing with Crystals, Gems, and Stones), and Credentialed Religious Educator. She is an educator, and spiritual activist with an eye on ecology, feminism, and green living ideas. With her neuro linguistic programming capabilities, she helps people change habits, such as smoking or nail biting.

Women who wish to lose weight, build confidence, find a mate, and many other life issues can benefit from coaching with NLP. She helps lead women into deeper spirituality, and she also speaks, writes, and leads workshops on such topics as spirituality, wellness, creativity, and other life issues.

Connie is available for one-on-one life coaching, specializing in spiritual, creative, and wellness issues. As a *Neuro-Linguistic Programmer* combined with *Life Coaching*, Connie has a myriad of different techniques that can help in all areas of life - professional and personal. Whether you want to deepen your spiritual self, build confidence, be more creative, reduce pain, break habits, and just live more intentionally, she can facilitate this in your life.

Connie also teaches workshops and classes that facilitate spiritual and creative growth, as well as encourages healing and deeper spiritual connections. These are taught at various locations.

For more than 25 years, Connie was a religious educator for Unitarian Universalist Churches. She has written curricula for children, youth and adults, as well as designed and led workshops, rituals, house blessings, and personal ceremonies.

As a journalist and magazine writer, she also brings in the elements of language, storytelling, poetry, freelance writing, writing for children, book writing (fiction, self- help, cookbook, and spiritual). She also develops workshops, curricula, illustrates some of her books, makes puppets, speaks and does many other things.

"It takes many lifetimes to develop everything you want to cram into life, so I honestly hope to come back again and again to continue my journey!" Connie says.

Connie's newest books:
- *TREES: Peaceful and Personal Meditational Poems*, a collection of meditative, nature poetry. To order, go to: http://www.trees-meditative.com
- *Goddess Rituals*, a book on how to create your own Goddess Rituals and understand Goddess Archetypes. To order, go to: http://goddessrituals.webs.com
- *The Most Magical, Awesome, Delicate Creature of All*, a children's story of the creation of butterflies. To order, go to: http://magicalawesomedelicatecreature.webs.com.

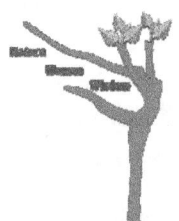

**Nature Woman Wisdom**
Connie Dunn, Holistic Healing Practitioner
http://www.naturewomanwisdom.com
naturewomanwisdom@gmail.com
508-446-1711

www.ingramcontent.com/pod-product-compliance
Lightning Source LLC
Chambersburg PA
CBHW080344170426
43194CB00014B/2682